D0960252

ISBN: 1-879-620-56-1

Please note: The information appearing in this publication is presented for educational purposes only. In no case shall the publishers or authors be held responsible for any use readers may choose to make, or not to make, of this information.

Belvoir Publications Inc.
Box 2626
75 Holly Hill Lane
Greenwich, CT 06836 USA

Lyons, John
Communicating with Cues:
The Rider's Guide to Training and Problem Solving Part II
 John Lyons with Maureen Gallatin

ISBN. 1-879-620-56-1
1. Horses - Training   2. Horsemanship   3. Horses

Manufactured in the United States of America

John Lyons' The Making of a Perfect Horse

Communicating with Cues:

The Rider's Guide to Training and Problem Solving
Part II

John Lyons with Maureen Gallatin

Belvoir Publications, Inc.
Greenwich, CT

Contents

Section I: Round Pen Principles

Choosing A Round Pen 11
John talks about what to look for and what to avoid.

Request, Response, Reward 19
*We have to know beforehand exactly what we expect from
ourselves and our horse.*

Getting Started In The Round Pen 31
*Our objective is to establish a cue and get a consistent response
from our horse, one small step at a time.*

Both Eyes Means Forward 41
*Looking at the trainer with both eyes is the basis for most all
ground training, including teaching our horse to come to us.*

Sacking Out: Not Just For Greenies 51
*Sacking out, like giving to the bit, is often misunderstood. Train
your horse to calmly cope with all kinds of scary stuff.*

First-Saddling Essentials 63
*Teaching this lesson can make you and your horse feel both safe
and confident the first time you climb onto his back.*

Spook In Place 73
*You can't expect your horse to never get scared, but you can
teach him what to do when he gets afraid.*

First Ride 83
*What you should do to help assure your horse's first ride will be
a great experience for both you and him*

Section II: Riding Problems Solved

The "Don't Shy" Cue 97
*Ironically, there's no cue to say, "Don't shy." So what are we to
tell our horse?*

A Horse's Attention: The Last Thing You'll Get 105
First comes the rider's concentration, then the rider's consistency,
then the horse's performance and, finally, the horse's attention.

Sweetie Pie And J. Seezher 113
Why horses kick each other on the trail, and what you can do to
see it coming, and prevent it happening.

Why A Snaffle Bit? 119
Bits are simply tools we use to communicate with our horses. So
why do we recommend a full cheek snaffle?

A Rear-Ending Lesson 127
Teach your horse a cue to put his head — and his feet — down,
without endangering yourself by getting on his back.

When Trail Riding Isn't Fun 143
What you do if you have "performance problems" on the trail but
don't have a trainer, arena or round pen to work in?

Section III: Trailer Loading Problems Solved
Checking Out A Trailer 153
John's recommendations about safety features and convenience
in horse trailers.

Trailer Loading 101 163
One four-hour lesson can yield a lifetime of safe and easy trailer
loading. The "go forward" cue is the secret.

Eliminating Escape Options 175
We'll show you how to fine-tune trailer loading and how to
improve your horse's ground-handling manners in the process.

Trailering Dilemmas 185
Trailering 101 is completed, and your horse loads easily, but then
problems develop. You need a plan.

Section IV: Putting Theory Into Practice
It Was Worth The Try 197
A success story: Te was afraid of people and hadn't been
handled since he was a weanling, until Dan decided to try.

Focus On Driving 201
World-class driver Keady Cadwell improves communication with
her horses using Lyons' techniques.

Index 207

Sweet talking won't do it.

Carrots won't do it.

You need a cue!

Preface

A wise man named "Solomon" once said that since a dull axe requires great strength, you should sharpen the blade. He went on to say that with wisdom and skills, you will succeed. And, that's what this book is all about — succeeding in horse training by developing specific cues — sharpening the axe blade. Since we can't outmuscle our 1,000-pound animal, we need another way to teach our horse.

We'll begin doing that in the round pen, teaching our horse to turn left and right even without a halter. We'll teach him to stand and face his fears when he gets scared, and we'll prepare him so that his first ride will be safe for both him and us. Once we've learned the principles of training that we use in the round pen, we can adapt those lessons for use anytime, with or without a pen. It's being specific in our expectations, cues and rewards that gives us that edge we can use to go on to solve riding problems. After that, we'll teach our horses to load in the trailer, so we will never have to risk injury by dealing with a horse who won't load safely. Then, just for fun and encouragement, we'll relate a couple of success stories. You'll learn how consistency on the part of the trainer produces consistently good performance by the horse.

As you sharpen your training skills, remember that God promises to give wisdom generously to all who ask for it.

May God bless you and your family and your perfect horses.

John Lyons

Praise the Lord, I tell myself, and never forget the good things He does for me. He forgives all my sins and heals all my diseases. He ransoms me from death and surrounds me with love and tender mercies
Psalm 103: 2-4

Section I

Principles
for
Round Pen Training
and Problem Solving

1

Choosing A Round Pen

With growing numbers of people investing in round pens, we asked John to talk with us about what to look for and what to avoid.

A round pen is going to be your horse's classroom, and like a classroom for children, it should be a safe environment in which the pupil can learn.

In fact, it was an accident that prompted me to look into providing safe, well-made round pens. In 1988, I was working a horse in a borrowed round pen, and as the horse ran alongside the fence, he cut his knee on a sharp edge on the center support bar of a portable panel. He was lame for life.

By then I'd already worked several thousand horses in many kinds of pens, and I knew what features make a pen safe. I determined never to risk a horse by borrowing equipment, and I had a manufacturer make one pen to my specifications, which I carried with me. I ended up getting so many inquiries about that pen, that I made arrangements to have more made at a reasonable cost.

Whether your round pen is to be pipe or any other material, keep these considerations in mind.

Dimensions of round pen

I find a 60-foot diameter is ideal — not so large that the horse or trainer has to work too hard, and not so small that the horse feels trapped or unwilling to move forward. And, at 60 feet, you can ride in it or work more than one horse at a time, if need be.

The materials and construction of your round pen should be such that the horse feels securely confined, and you feel confident the horse won't get hurt if he challenges the fence.

The sides should be six feet high; any shorter is inviting trouble. When you use a five-foot fence, commonly you have to deal with the horse thinking about jumping or scrambling over it. The pen becomes a distraction rather than a help.

You want the footing to be safe. It should be about two inches deep and over a firm base. If you use deep sand, you risk injury to the horse, and it makes working too difficult for both the horse and the trainer. If the ground is too hard, the concussion on the horse's feet and legs is too much. Periodically drag the surface so you don't end up with the softer footing banked against the fence and the "track" becoming too hard.

The gate should be wide, preferably six feet or more. It is difficult to bring a saddled horse through a narrower gate without bumping it, possibly frightening him or getting a stirrup caught. Ideally, the gate should swing both ways, allowing you to push the gate and swing it out of the way from either side.

If you use a pipe gate with a top rail, it should be tall enough so that the horse and rider can safely pass through. Eight feet is ideal. Less than that will work, particularly if you don't ride through it, but I wouldn't recommend it.

The gate latch should be flush to the fence, not sticking out. It should not have any protruding edges, whether the gate is open or closed. It should be easy for people to open from either side, but not easy for a horse to open.

ROUND PENS HOLD THEIR VALUE REMARKABLY WELL. IN FACT, ONE OF THE MAJOR SELLING FEATURES OF A GOOD PORTABLE ROUND PEN IS THAT IT CAN BE RESOLD OR MOVED.

Portable pipe pens

There are countless numbers of pipe pens available commercially, and some folks choose to make their own from various types of pipe material. This chapter is not a plug for the portable pipe pens that I sell; but, by looking at the features I've incorporated into my product, you'll know what I think is important.

One of the key factors to keep in mind is that you will be working your horse in the pen, not just fencing him in. Standard pipe corral panels are not recommended for round-pen use for safety reasons, as I'll explain later.

Don't cut costs by getting pipe that is too narrow or has sharp edges. It should be two inches or more in diameter. Smaller-diameter pipe is generally weaker and not as safe. The thinner pipe is more likely to dent, causing a sharp edge, which could injure a horse or further weaken the fence. Should a horse bang into the "fatter" pipe, the impact is distributed over a greater surface, reducing the risk of injury.

One of the most important safety concerns is that the center support brace be made of the same two-inch pipe as the rest of the pen, and form-fitted for strength. Here's where most companies cut costs, and our horses end up paying the difference.

At some point you'll end up with a horse standing on a rail of the fence, though it may be hard to believe if you haven't experienced it. You'll have left the horse in the pen alone while you go to the barn. He'll start pawing and before long the rail is bearing his weight. You'll want to be sure the pipe is supported well enough that it's not going to pull away from the posts or bow in the middle.

Because pipe panels are manufactured to serve a variety of livestock markets, often the bars are close together so animals do not escape. But when working a horse, it is important that if he puts a foot through the bars, there is enough room for him to withdraw his foot again easily. The bars should also be far enough apart that if he puts his head through the bars, he can pull it out again easily.

You don't want rounded corners on the top of the panels. **While rounding the corners may sound like a good idea, in reality, if a horse gets his foot up near the top corner, the rounded shape guides the foot down between the two panels where it is likely to get stuck.** You want the corners of the panels to be close together and squared off.

You'll want the bottom rail at a height no closer to the ground than 16 inches. As the horse goes around the pen, his feet are often quite close the edge of the fence, sometimes even stepping outside the pen under the panel. And, when we turn our horses out in the round pen and they roll, you want to be sure they can't get their feet stuck.

I prefer a kicker-leg panel to a straight-leg design, but it should have a large loop to rest on. With the small loop, the bottom rail is generally too close to the ground, and it's easy for the horse to get a leg caught in the loop. The large loop provides added support to the corner of the panel and eliminates the necessity of a bar at ground level.

Convenience factors

Easy care may be important. Painted steel panels rust quickly and require painting every few years to look good. Galvanized pipe requires little maintenance. Both steel and galvanized pipe are heavy.

So if you are planning for your round pen to be portable, or if you want to be able to move it for ease of mowing, we'd opt for aluminized steel. It is almost as strong as steel but about one-third the weight, and it's relatively maintenance-free.

You'll want an easy way to disassemble your pen, if it's to be portable. A clamp system of holding the rails together is time-consuming to work with, and the close tolerances generally demand that the pen be on level ground. **I prefer drop-pinned panels because they can be taken apart quickly**, which is important should

Round pen panels can be configured in many ways. I prefer panels that rest on large kick loops, which make it easy for a horse to withdraw his foot should he paw and put it through the fence.

a horse get hung up, and they are not so dependent on the terrain being flat.

Because our panels are lightweight and easy to move, Susie and I take them camping with us and use them as temporary stalls when folks come to visit with their horses.

Wooden round pens

Whether to fit into the look of your ranch or because of the availability of materials, some folks prefer a wooden round pen. Wooden pens can be beautiful and functional as well. Be sure the walls are two inches thick or more, so they have enough strength, and use treated lumber.

Unlike with portable pipe pens, there should be no space between the bottom board and the ground. If a horse stepped under the board, he risks injury from the sharp board edge.

The sides of the pen should be straight up, not slanted outward. The bottom panel should be wide, so I suggest using a 2" x 10" or 2" x 12" and placing it horizontally on the ground. Allow two inches of space, then another 2" x 12", another two inches of space, another 2" x 12", and so forth. You want that space in between the panels so air comes into the pen, but you don't want the space big enough that a horse can get himself into trouble.

I recommend the pen have a span of 10-foot or between posts. The posts, of course, should be on the outside and be substantial, so you have plenty to nail to. Like the pipe pens, the wooden pen should be six feet high. The top "rail" of the pen should be smooth all around, with no posts showing above.

Make the gate as solid as you can and have it look the same as the rest of the pen. Many people make the mistake of building a beautiful wooden round pen, then using a pipe-corral gate. If you make the gate more open-looking than the rest of the pen, you'll create a problem for yourself and your horse.

Metal pens

Metal pens are generally safer than pipe panels, unless the top rails are close together, as you can see in the photo on the left. If a horse gets a foot caught, it is very difficult to free him.

The sides should be tall and straight, not slanted. Horses tend to try to run up the slanted sides of a metal pen and risk falling. The only real drawback to metal pens is they are expensive and not portable.

Used pens

Round pens hold their value remarkably well. In fact, one of the major selling features of a good portable round pen is that it can be resold or moved, should you change locations. Don't

We tied Seattle to the outside of this metal round pen. For maximum safety, the metal sides should be taller and the top rails farther apart.

The same advice applies to wooden round pens as to the metal pens. You can see how, if this horse reared close to the fence, he might risk catching a foot in the top rail.

overlook the possibility that a good used round pen may be available in your area. That would save you some money in freight and give you the opportunity of checking out each of its features.

There's no magic in the round pen itself — no matter who makes it. But it is a helpful tool and, for many folks, well worth the investment. ⊞

Notes

2

Request, Response, Reward

To lay the foundation for round-pen work,
we have to know beforehand
exactly what we expect from ourselves and our horse.

TRUE OR FALSE?

Common thinking about round-pen training:

- You have to do round-pen work in a round pen.
- If the horse follows the trainer around, then the trainer is in control.
- Round-pen training is just for "unbroke" horses.

The objective of round-pen training is:

- To wear the horse down until he finally decides that if he stands by the trainer he can rest.
- To get the horse to follow the trainer.
- To tire the horse out so he has less fight.
- To let the horse know that the trainer is tougher than the horse.

All Are False!

All round-pen training methods are not alike, and misinformation about training in the round pen abounds. When we speak of doing round-pen work, we are talking about using specific training principles, not just working a horse in a small, circular corral. "Round pen" is essentially a set of training lessons, not a place. Round-pen training gives us a means of establishing control of our horse, while minimizing the risk of injury to the horse or to us.

Whenever we ask our horse to do something, we want him do it without hesitation. Willing responsiveness keeps us safe. Because

When the horse is on the end of a lead line, the trainer is "attached" to him. With an untrained horse, this can be unsafe. Round pen work gives us a way to establish a language with our horse without being so close to him as to risk injury.

horses are big, strong and agile, safety dictates that we remain in control, not the horse. It is our responsibility to teach the horse a system of signals for us to communicate with him so he knows how to respond to our requests.

The horse learns a pattern of request, right response, then reward. That is why it is important to be systematic and consistent. Spending time on the most elementary request, and getting that response and reward down pat, means that the horse knows a reward always awaits his doing the right thing.

To evaluate any training program, and whenever I work through a training session, I always use three rules:

1. The trainer cannot get hurt.
2. The horse cannot get hurt.
3. The horse should be calmer at the end of the lesson than he was at the beginning.

Safety is always the No. 1 concern when beginning any training program. **The less well-trained the horse, the more important it is to control the environment where you work with him.** I believe the safest place to begin training a horse is in a round pen. If you begin a horse's training at the end of a lead line, you and he are "attached." He can't get away from you, but neither can you get away from him, which means you may not be safe if the horse panics or gets aggressive.

There's no magic in the pen itself, nor in using a round-shaped pen. But with no corners where the horse can get "stuck," the round pen always gives the horse a place to go. When horses feel trapped, accidents are more likely to happen.

You can use the conditioned-response round-pen lessons with any horse, pony or mule, regardless of his history, age, breed, sex or temperament. You need not be an experienced horseman to follow this system. However, as with anything, the more experience you have, the easier it becomes. **If, during the course of working with your horse in the round pen, you find yourself confused or frightened, stop**. You can even leave the pen, get a drink of water and think it over. You can quit at any time. **No matter when you quit, the horse will not have "gotten away with" anything.**

It's important to know specifically what you want the horse to do before getting in the pen with him. I say this because many trainers use round pens, but not all round-pen training is the same. Unless your objectives are clear, it's easy to lump the methods together and confuse yourself and your horse.

As valuable as round-pen work is, I only use the round pen for a few days in the horse's life, as a tool to establish control and teach specific lessons. Folks use round pens for many uses, from turnout to training to riding, but the initial round-pen lessons are something that once the horse learns, you don't have to reteach. When I am confident that I have good control of the horse, and that he'll obey me despite distractions, then I can safely take him outside the round-pen environment to continue his training.

If the horse is halter-trained, safe to handle, and under good control, you can do many of the same lessons on a lead line.

Objectives

If we do the round-pen work correctly, several changes will occur even in the first session.

■ *The horse will physically do what we ask. He may not appear to pay attention to us — he may not even look at us initially, but he will learn to move his feet in the direction we want. That's the beginning of control.*

■ *Not only will he move his feet where we ask, but he'll learn to do it consistently. When you get consistent response, you've made a breakthrough. The horse is beginning to understand your signal; he's not just "lucking into" the right answer.*

■ *The horse's fear level will go down. When he's less afraid, he can think better. A horse doesn't learn well when he's scared.*

■ *You will build confidence in your ability to signal the horse and get a response. You'll also have more confidence in your safety, not because you are more brave, but because, if the horse comes too close to you, you'll have a signal to tell him to move away.*

■ *You will establish a pattern that you can follow for all the horse's training: Make a request, he responds correctly, you reward him.*

■ *The horse will see you as the boss and develop confidence in your direction. As his performance improves, he will start to pay more attention to you.*

■ *As he pays more attention to you, you can teach him new lessons.*

Before we go much further, I want to clear up any misconceptions you may have about what happens in the round pen. We don't run the horse until he learns that he can rest if he stands still or comes to us. And, we don't work the horse so hard that he "gives up" out of fatigue.

Motivation

How many people would pay taxes on time if there wasn't a penalty or an April 15 deadline? And how many teenagers automatically clean up their room just because they love us or because we provide them with dinner? Not many. It doesn't work that way with our horses, either.

So the first thing we must do is give the horse a good reason to do what we want him to do. For a motivator to be effective, it must

Beyond establishing basic control, the round pen can facilitate teaching advanced lessons, including halterless leading.

be something that makes sense to him. **As much as we'd like to think that our untrained horse will do something for love, food, praise, petting or even getting over his fear, those things are not strong enough motivators at the beginning of his training.** We might use them later on when he doesn't need as much motivation, but at the beginning, they are not important enough to him for him to change his behavior.

What immediately makes sense to the horse is his "rank" in the pecking order. We see this in action in a pasture when a dominant horse approaches a water trough where another horse is standing. The submissive horse discreetly steps away, recognizing who is the boss. Building on the horse's innate understanding of hierarchy, we'll set up a scenario in which the horse gets the idea that the trainer outranks him. We can do this in the round pen without using any kind of force or abuse. **Once a horse recognizes that you are controlling not only his movement but also the direction of movement, without causing any external physical pain to his body, he will begin to respect and trust you.**

The second factor that makes sense to him is rest from work. **No matter how spirited the horse, deep down he's lazy.** So letting him rest is a reward he'll recognize. As he gets slightly out of breath — not tired or exhausted, just the feeling you would have if you ran up a flight of stairs — he'll look for ways to stop working. As he looks to us, we'll be able to help him out. Pretty soon he'll figure out what he did to get us to help him. As this happens, he develops trust in us and realizes we won't abuse him or overwork him, and he learns that specific actions merit specific responses.

Equipment and preparation

I always use leg protection on my horse. As the horse turns, he could hit one leg with his opposite hoof or bang his leg into the side of the pen. In addition to eliminating the chance of injury whenever we can, we don't want the horse to experience any pain. **Pain from any source is always a distraction from the lesson.**

You'll also need a lunge whip or a 30-foot soft lariat, which will become an extension of your arm. I prefer the rope, as I have good control of it and can make it any length I need.

Regardless of which tool you choose, minimize its use. As you watch videos of me working in the round pen, you'll see that I use the rope only enough to get the desired response. For instance, if I want the horse to move away, and he does that when I raise the coiled rope, then I don't do anything more with the rope than that.

Although the rope is used to signal the horse, we don't want him to be afraid of it.

The levels of stimulation that I use with the rope are:
- Raise the coiled rope
- Wave it in the air
- Slap my leg with the coiled rope
- Toss the rope halfway to the horse, letting it uncoil as it goes
- Toss it all the way to the horse (uncoiled)
- Toss it uncoiled and hit the horse's hip with the end of rope.

Whenever you throw the lariat, coil it up immediately so you have it available again.

SAFETY IS ALWAYS THE NO. 1 CONCERN

WHEN BEGINNING ANY TRAINING PROGRAM.

THE LESS WELL-TRAINED THE HORSE,

THE MORE IMPORTANT IT IS TO

CONTROL THE ENVIRONMENT WHERE

YOU WORK WITH HIM.

One of the most valuable aids is the "kiss." **When I make a kissing sound to the horse, I'm telling him, "Move something."** Sometimes it just means, "Move your head so both eyes can focus on me." Of course, the horse doesn't know what the kiss means at first, so I'll use something else (like the rope) at the same time as the kiss. When he moves, I stop kissing. If he doesn't move, I keep kissing. If I stopped kissing before he does what I want, I would be telling him that the kiss is a random thing with no significance. So consistency in your movements is key to developing a communication system with your horse.

As I kiss to him, I focus on what I'm asking him to do. If I'm asking him to go forward, I'll kiss to him, focusing on the top of his hip. If he doesn't respond to my kiss, I'll follow up immediately with the rope as I keep kissing and focusing on that cue spot. The logical next question is, "John, if you kiss to turn his head left and kiss to go forward, how does the horse know what your kiss means? How are you cueing him?"

John is "putting pressure" on Zip's nose. To the casual observer, John's cues may seem general. To Zip, they are specific.

Developing cue spots

We don't ask the whole horse to do anything. **If we can control one part of his body, we can control the whole horse. This is a key concept, not just for round-pen work, but even through to upper-level training.** For instance, when I ride Zip, I use the rein to talk with specific spots, asking him to move his right foot right or to take the left lead. **In the round pen, when you ask the horse's hip to go forward, the hip will push the rest of the horse into motion.**

Initially, our cues will be relatively obvious, such as throwing the rope toward the horse, moving to different positions in the round pen or waving our arms. We'll use physical movement, along with the kiss and our focus on the cue spot. As we become consistent, our horse will no longer need all three signals to understand what we want, and a more subtle focus on the cue spot will get the desired response.

Have you ever tried to get someone's attention just by looking directly at them? By keeping your focus on them, without even waving your arms or calling their name, some people would become aware of your attention after awhile and look your way. Well, horses are much more aware of subtleties in body language than people, so this technique works for us in training, once the horse knows to look to us for signals.

To ask for movement, we will use three main cue spots or control points. I often use a livestock paint marker and actually mark a spot for my horse's nose cue spot (technically the jaw by the corner of his lips), the point of his shoulder and his hip. That way, I train myself to "talk" to each spot. The three spots are:

■ The top of the hip.
■ The nose.
■ The shoulder.

At first, you'll use only the spot on the top of the hip. This is the same spot for teaching the horse the cue to go forward for lungeing or trailer-loading, after he's learned the round-pen lessons. It tells the horse to step forward.

We'll speak of using this spot as "putting pressure on the hip." **When we put pressure on the horse's hip, we focus our line of vision, our body language and our rope or whip on that spot to signal to the horse that we want that hip to move forward.** As soon as the horse moves forward, we "release" him from that focus. For responsiveness on both sides, we'll have to work both the left- and right-hip cue spots.

After the horse clearly understands that cue, we'll next ask for a turn, by focusing on his nose. **At first, "putting pressure on the nose" means our body language will initially "herd" him to turn away**

John is "putting pressure on the hip," but not "chasing" Zip.

from us. In time, he'll understand more subtle language, and a mere focus on his nose with our look or raised rope, with the intent of asking him to turn away, will suffice.

These spots can be used with the trainer still 15 feet away from the horse. In fact, initially the trainer should maintain that distance for his own safety and so that the horse doesn't feel crowded.

Later on, we'll use a cue at the horse's shoulder to ask for a bend in his body or neck for more sophisticated work.

When to stop working

The rule I follow is, "**When you think you should stop working, you should.**" That means if you have a hunch that the horse is tired or can't safely handle additional work, your hunch may well be right. If you haven't overdone it today, you can always work him again to-morrow. If you suspect your horse may have a physical problem, like lameness, stop working him and call your veterinarian.

YOU NEED NOT BE AN EXPERIENCED
HORSEMAN TO FOLLOW THIS SYSTEM.
HOWEVER, AS WITH ANYTHING, THE MORE
EXPERIENCE YOU HAVE, THE EASIER IT
BECOMES.

Keep in mind that the round pen is a classroom and the horse is your pupil. **A young horse, such as a weanling, should go no more than three trips around the pen before resting.** Overworking your horse can damage his lungs. He needs to take breathers, literally. Also, consider the footing. In deep footing, muscles tire and tendons strain. Hard footing can be brutal on bones and joints, particularly for young or old horses.

When working for several hours, you may want to take a break and give your horse a drink. You may have to bring a bucket of water into the pen and leave the pen yourself, so the horse feels it's

OK to drink. If it's hot outside, watch that the horse isn't getting dehydrated. If your horse is breathing hard, sweating or lathered, you know that he is working hard. You don't want him to work hard for more than 20 minutes at a time, and that may be too long, depending on the horse's condition and the weather. Allow sufficient rest periods.

Don't change trainers in the middle of a training session. I never have someone spell me, even if I'm working a long time with a horse. If you are getting tired, it's likely that your horse is, too. If you are having difficulty, let the horse cool down and put him away. Try again later or ask someone for advice.

By repetition, your horse will learn the formula: Our request plus his correct response equals his reward. Not a bad deal. Beginning with basic forward movement, we'll teach our horse to consistently give us a "yes" answer to our questions and to get in the habit of cooperating with us.

And, if you have been riding or showing your horse for years and you think he wouldn't benefit from such basic work, you'll be amazed how going back to basics will improve his performance in many other ways. Most of all, you'll have the satisfaction of helping your horse develop an "I-want-to-please" attitude. ▣

Notes

3

Getting Started
In The Round Pen

*As we move into the round pen, our objective is
to establish a cue and get a consistent response
from our horse, one small step at a time.*

The preparation is complete. Your horse is wearing leg protection, and you've just turned him loose in the round pen. Now what? **If he is excited, running around or calling to his friends, give him a chance to settle down.** You may even have to leave the pen before he'll relax. Most horses settle after a few minutes, but for others, just getting comfortable in the pen is all you might expect the first day.

As he's settling down, review your objectives and guidelines:

■ You are your horse's teacher. Forget "horse training." Think "classroom" and treat your horse as you would a kindergarten pupil.

■ You can stop at any point. It does not mean the horse is "getting away" with anything.

■ If the horse isn't responding to your request, he's not being stupid or trying to make you look bad. It doesn't matter if he gave you the right response yesterday or 40 times today — if he doesn't give the correct response consistently, he hasn't learned the lesson.

■ You are not going to worry about training the whole horse. You only want specific spots of the horse to go specific directions. The rest will follow.

■ Only ask questions that your horse can answer "yes" to. We want our horse in the habit of getting along with us.

■ The clearer you tell your horse when he gets the right answer, the faster the training will progress.

First get the horse's feet to move. Here John is directing his lariat to the hip cue spot to ask the horse to go forward.

■ The more steps or little goals you can put in the training, the faster the horse will learn.
■ Accept improvement. It leads to consistent performance.
■ Preserve both your and the horse's energy. A tired pupil has a hard time concentrating.

Get the feet to move

Now both of you are ready. I'll walk you through the first part of the lesson as if I were working a horse. The first objective is to get the horse's feet moving. To do this, I generally raise my lariat and "put pressure on the hip," staying somewhat behind the horse and focusing my attention on the top of his hip.

It's usually pretty easy to get the horse to move. I use the least amount of stimulation possible. If the horse will move when I wave toward his hip, I don't unfurl the rope. If I can stand relatively still and get him to move, I don't hustle after him. He doesn't have to move off at a gallop — he just has to get his feet moving. A trot is ideal.

As I ask the horse to move, I make a kissing sound. **The kiss will become an important part of my communication with the horse. It** means, "Move something." In time, he'll figure out that when I kiss to him, I want him to move a part of his body, usually forward. For now, he won't know what it means; I only use it now to begin conditioning his response.

The rule I follow is: First get the feet to move, then get them to move consistently, then get them to move in the direction I want. With that in mind, I get the horse moving forward.

Now if it happens that the horse moves on his own, who is in control? He is. So if he moves on his own at three miles per hour, ask him to step it up to five mph for three or four strides. This is an important concept, because the horse occasionally lucks into a movement that we want. But, if he hasn't done it in response to our request, we are not in control.

If he seems aggressive

If you have a horse who is aggressive, or who you think may be aggressive, you'll want to take special precautions. Begin where you have control of the horse — you may not even start the round-pen work in a round pen.

For instance, assuming he's halter-broken, put a halter and lead rope on the horse and practice leading lessons with him. Using a dressage whip, teach him the "go forward" cue and work with him as if on a two-inch lunge line, so you have control of his head.

If you are concerned that he may bite, you can put a basket (muzzle) on him, which will prevent him from getting a hold of you with his teeth. However, it will not keep him from striking or otherwise being aggressive. In fact, sometimes when a horse can't bite, he gets even more angry. While neither a striking nor biting horse is safe, biting is the most dangerous thing a horse can do, because it's almost impossible to protect yourself. Also, realize that you can be injured when he slings his head around.

*If you are working the horse in the round pen, **do not work on inside turns until you have good control of the horse doing outside turns.** You do not want to encourage his coming toward you until you can tell the horse to take his nose away from you if he seems threatening.*

If I'm working with a horse and I have a hunch he might charge me, I back off on my requests and ease myself out of the situation. I don't want to challenge the horse or put him in a situation in which he feels he has to get aggressive to take care of himself.

If he does make an aggressive move toward you, throw your rope toward his face, pushing him away as quickly as possible. If you think he is aggressive and you don't feel you can handle him, or if you are concerned about the risk of injury, get help from someone who has experience.

Any time I make a move with a horse, I evaluate what I think are the chances of success, and what are the possibilities for injury. I always play it safe. *I don't want to bluff a horse and have him call the bluff.*

If the horse is just a little grumpy, with ears back and a lousy attitude, but not aggressive, I can often work him out of it. I'll become more aggressive with the rope, asking for direction changes more often and quickly. But it takes experience to know if you can work a horse through that stage or if you'll end up making him angry.

You can always break the lesson down into smaller and smaller steps, and thereby establish control without angering the horse, because you give him a release each time he does the smallest step correctly. *For instance, rather than asking for a complete turn, ask the horse to step forward, then stop, then forward, then stop, looking slightly to the outside of the pen, until you can ask for the complete outside turn or any part of it.*

Going left

Do each lesson step to the left first, and do the steps in sequence, so you always know where you are in the training. You may find yourself breaking a step down into smaller steps, which is fine, but don't rearrange the sequence of the exercise.

So, using the mildest stimulus you can, as we discussed earlier, get the horse moving left (counterclockwise) — that is, with his left side closest to you. After he travels around the pen to the left a few times, he may try to change direction. When he does, focus attention on the point of his left hip, and quickly move toward the fence behind him, cutting him off and encouraging him to continue to the left.

In the event that he completes the turn, step toward the fence to block his path, asking him to change back. **The quicker you turn him so he's going left again, the quicker he will get the message that you want him to go left.** Having said that, remember you want a change of direction, not a crisis, so use common sense. If you are not able to turn him back, take your time and do it the next time he comes around.

Your first big objective is to get the horse traveling left without trying to change directions. If you get lucky and the horse travels left without trying to change directions, don't make the mistake of thinking you're in control. Up until the time that the horse tries to change direction on his own, he has no idea that you are controlling him. If he moved away in response to your initial "shooing," he'll think moving was his idea. It's only when he makes a decision to do something (like change direction) and you tell him to do something else that he gets the idea.

Going right

To ask the horse to change directions when the horse is moving left, step toward the fence at a spot where his nose will be in few strides, while looking at his nose (putting pressure on the nose). At the same time, make the kissing sound. It doesn't matter which way he turns, but most horses will turn to the outside (toward the fence). As soon as he turns, relax your posture, stop kissing and step back toward the center of the round pen, telling him that he did want you wanted. **The quicker you can give him the "that's right" signal, the quicker he'll learn.**

If he doesn't change directions, step aside and let him go by. You cannot force the horse to change direction, and you don't want to get into a wreck. Just keep working with it until the horse does what you want. If you can't get the horse to turn, then walk to the fence and stand there. In order not to run you over, he'll change directions. When that happens, calmly walk to the middle of the pen and tell him soothingly that he did a good job. If he didn't turn when you were just standing there, flap your arms like a chicken or do

Use only the minimum energy required. Here John uses body language to ask for an outside turn. Then he asks the horse to continue moving to the right.

some other big movement so he moves away from you (and hopefully changes direction). But, only use the level of stimulation that you need — don't overdo it.

Now the horse should be going to the right. Follow the same plan you used in having him go left. When he tries to turn back to the left, cut him off and send him right again, each time remembering that your signal to go forward is to focus on his hip spot. You are establishing a cue, so you have to be consistent.

If you find you can't send the horse back to the right as we've described — and you are handy with the lariat — you can toss it a few strides in front of his path to encourage him to pause and change direction.

Now ask the horse to change direction from the right, just as you did when he was going left.

ACCEPT IMPROVEMENT. IT LEADS TO

CONSISTENT PERFORMANCE.

Inside and outside turns

There are two types of direction changes — inside turns (toward the center of the round pen) and outside turns (toward the fence). You want to develop the inside turn first, unless your horse may be aggressive, in which case outside turns should be taught first.

For an outside turn, you're going to "put pressure on the nose" asking the horse's nose to go toward the fence, as you see me doing on the previous page. **Then, when the nose has made the turn, "put pressure on the hip," asking it to move forward, so that the horse completes the turn.** It may help you to point to the cue spot with your finger to get your signals consistent.

Realize that the horse needs space to turn. **When you ask for a change of direction, don't crowd him, which may make him feel like his options are to be pinned against the fence or run past you.** You want to move toward the fence in front of him to block his nose, but you don't want him to end up crashing the fence.

To get an inside turn, step toward the fence behind you, or to the side, giving his nose lots of room, while kissing to him. Instead of your body language chasing his nose away, it invites him to come toward you. If the horse turns to the outside, cut him off and get him moving the same direction again, and again ask for an inside turn.

He's already learned that when he turns he is rewarded by not having to do anything for a few strides. **But, when you ask for an inside turn and he gives you the outside turn, and you immediately turn him back the other way**, he'll realize he didn't give you the right answer. He'll experiment to find out what you want.

John asked for an inside turn, but the horse attemped to turn to the outside. John quickly pushed him forward to complete the inside turn.

After a few times, he'll try an inside turn. When he does, step away from him, giving him extra room, which lets him know he made the right decision.

Getting specific

In every lesson, we accept a movement, then improve on it. So we want to develop control over when and where the horse turns, just as you'll want control over where and how quickly the horse turns and stops when you ride him. And, just as we told specific parts of the horse's body to turn, it's only logical that we pick specific locations for him to turn. I recommend you put cones or buckets at points outside the pen to act as markers.

Send your horse left and ask him for an outside turn at cone No. 1, which you can place anywhere except by the gate. If he turns, but not until cone No. 6, you know that next time you should begin your request earlier. **You want his nose to turn specifically at the cone.**

When you can get him to turn from the left at No. 1, then ask him at cone No. 6, then at No. 4 and so forth, each time letting him know when he did what you wanted. You don't want to repeat any one cone more than three times before going on to another.

When you can get the outside turn from the left, by cueing the horse on his nose and hips spots, then do the same lesson with the horse moving to the right. Then, ask for inside turns at various cones from the left, then from the right. Then vary the sequence of turns, asking for a left inside turn, then a right outside turn and so forth. All of this can be done at any gait. But, if your horse isn't responding at the walk or trot, it may be that he's still pretty scared. **Reduce the intensity without changing your objectives.**

By now you should have a great sense of accomplishment, because you've developed a cue language, you've taught your horse the language, and he's responding consistently.

FOR AN OUTSIDE TURN, YOU'RE GOING TO "PUT PRESSURE ON THE NOSE" ASKING THE HORSE'S NOSE TO GO TOWARD THE FENCE

Getting a stop

Your next objective is to get the horse to stop while facing the fence. Up until now, you've only asked him to move. He has to learn that it's OK to just stand where you want him to stand.

Ask him to go left, then ask for an outside turn. After he travels halfway around the pen, ask for another outside turn. When he's gone about one-third of the way around, request another outside turn.

John asks the horse to stop using a series of outside turns, with less distance between turns. When the horse stops, John lets him stand and relax. He has to learn it's OK not to move.

Continue this pattern, making the distance he travels shorter and shorter. As the distance between the turns gets shorter, you'll see the horse's outside hind foot stop for a moment, then for longer periods. **Each time you see that foot stop, pause before asking the horse to move, offering him the chance to stop if he wants to.**
When the horse stops moving, immediately step away from him, letting him know he guessed the right answer, and letting him know it's OK to stand there. If he moves again on his own, repeat the sequence of outside turns until he's again stopped. Step away from him and allow him to relax standing. ▣

4

Both Eyes Means Forward

*Looking at the trainer with both eyes
is a forward-motion exercise.
It's the basis for most all ground training,
including teaching our horse to come to us.*

Now our horse is trained to make inside and outside turns, and to stop facing the fence. Our next objective is to get him to stop parallel to the fence using a combination of cues. Although we'll use a number of steps in our lesson plan, they fall into two categories: **teaching the horse to stand as we approach him and teaching him to approach us.** In order to help him understand what we want, we're going to be downright nit-picky specific. Just asking him to turn and face us is a general request. **And a general — or vague — request gives us a general response. We want specific movements from our horse.**

First, we'll ask for an outside turn. Then, before the horse makes the full turn, we'll back off on our cue, allowing him to stop with only a partial turn made. This may not happen automatically, but building on the stop lesson and a combination of inside and outside turns, you can get the horse to stop parallel to the fence instead of facing into it.

If you wanted a full turn, you'd keep "pressure" on the cue spot until the turn is completed, as you did earlier. **But, when you back off, the horse will know he's turned far enough. When you've done this enough times, he'll recognize the difference between your asking him for a complete outside turn or just a step in that direction.**

Now he's probably stopped angled toward the fence. Kiss to him, asking for the beginning of an inside turn. He'll probably look at you, which may be all you can expect at first. If he turns his head to look at you, back off, letting him know he's on the right track.

Again kiss to him, this time asking him to move his feet as if making an inside turn. If the horse moves toward the inside beyond where he's parallel to the fence, block his movement, as you did for an outside turn, to get him to stop parallel to the fence. This will require some finesse — kissing and working the hip and nose spots until the horse is stopped parallel to the fence. When the horse is in position, walk away from him, back to the center of the pen. Allow him to stand, as you did when he was facing the fence. You want him to know that's all you are asking of him.

Now you are in the middle of the pen and the horse is standing parallel to the fence. If the horse moves forward, signal him to stop and reposition him. **If he moves back, immediately ask him to step forward. We don't want any backward steps or thoughts.** If he looks toward you, let him look. If he looks outside the pen, kiss to him, asking him to look toward you, and ask him to move forward again. Reposition him parallel to the fence.

Now to face you

Assuming the horse is facing slightly outside or parallel to the fence, would it be easier for him to face you if you were in the middle of the pen, or if you stepped in front of him? Obviously, if you reposition yourself, it's easier for the horse. So that's how we'll begin, with the horse positioned parallel to the fence. **Since we do every exercise to the left first, have him begin facing left, that is, with his right side to the fence.**

Walk to where you can face the horse head on, but about 10 to 15 feet in front of him. Until now, when we moved toward the horse it signaled him to move. **So we have to show him that we only want him to stand looking at us. This is a definite step in the training — not just something that automatically happens.**

If the horse moves when you get 14 feet from him, then stop at least 15 feet away. Each time he moves away, reposition him, then reposition yourself.

Both eyes on you

When the horse looks at you with both eyes, it is a forward-motion exercise. When he turns his head away from you (or maybe he's never looked right at you up to this point), kiss to him to get his attention. Your objective is to condition him to look at you with both eyes every

To begin teaching the horse to look at him with both eyes, John positions himself on the rail. He then steps toward the center of the pen. The horse's gaze should follow him.

When the horse turns his head away from John, John kisses and moves the rope, asking for the horse to look at him, ready to ask him to move if he doesn't.

time you are in the pen or pasture with him. By focusing on the hip cue spot with your eyes, and making whatever noise (kissing) or motion (wave of the lariat) you need to in order to get the horse to look at you, you ask him to look at you with both eyes. You essentially ask him to go forward, but with his eyes, not his feet.

This step is extremely important. If you were at one of my symposiums, I would tell you to underline, circle and double-star the following point in your notes: **Looking at you with both eyes is a forward-motion exercise. The more fear your horse has, the more important it is to get him to look at you with both eyes.** At a later time, when you try to approach him with the saddle blanket or saddle, you may have a hard time if he hasn't learned to think "forward" and to look "forward."

As soon as he looks at you with both his eyes, stop the kissing and motion, relax your posture, and just let him look. When he moves his head up, down or anywhere else, ask him to look at you again. After just a moment, turn and walk away from the horse, leaving him with an "Is that all you wanted?" expression on his face.

If, while he's supposed to be looking at you, the horse looks back, leans back or looks like he's thinking "back," immediately kiss to him and ask him to step forward and look at you again. **When he's thinking "back," he's protecting himself from you. He's backing up in his mind, even if his feet haven't moved yet.** If you don't interrupt his thought and replace it with a forward thought (by getting him to step forward or to look at you again), you'll be encouraging his wrong line of thinking.

The kiss means move

Remember, we're using the kiss sound to mean "move something." At this stage, I want him to move his head so he can look at me with both eyes. **If I kiss to him and he doesn't move his head to look at me within two seconds, then I'll have to get him to move something else, like his feet. If I don't, then I'm teaching him the kiss means "don't move."**

A bend in the neck

Have you ever heard a person described as stiff-necked? They are hard to work with, stuck in their own line of thinking. That expression is more than just a cliché; it's reality. We don't want stiff-necked horses. For some reason, the better you do this next exercise, the more control you develop and the better the rest of the training seems to go. (Think about a horse dragging someone off at the end of the lead rope. The first thing he does is stiffen his neck and look away from the handler.)

When you can consistently get your horse to look at you with both eyes, step toward the center of the arena, encouraging him to bend his neck. Your horse should continue to look at you. Continue to take steps, one at a time, asking the horse to look at you for longer periods. If he looks away, immediately call his attention back as you did before. If he persists in not looking at you, ask him to step forward, then begin the exercise again.

Pretend you are sitting where the horse is, on the rail, and bending your neck to watch a TV in the middle of the pen. Before long, your neck would get tired. So, you'd walk across the arena, pick up the whole entertainment center so it faces correctly, then return to your chair on the rail — Not! You'd turn your chair so your shoulders squared up to the TV. Because your neck got tired, you moved your feet. That's what happens with your horse. **As the horse's neck begins to tire, he'll take his nose forward. Immediately ask him to look at you again. In time, he'll turn his feet to face you.**

This part is almost like a dance. As you step toward the middle, sometimes the horse will follow you with his eyes, but then he'll want to look forward again. As soon as he does, step toward his head again and kiss to him. When he looks back at you, relax. Then take another step toward the middle, ask him to look at you with both eyes, and so forth.

Can you imagine how neat it would be if, before you even halter-trained a horse, you had a cue that would prevent him from pulling away from you? Imagine how much easier halter-training and leading lessons would be. By doing this exercise well, should the horse begin to pull away when you are leading him, you can call his eyes to you, then lead him where you want, without tension on you or the rope.

The nose will move the feet

Someplace along the way, you'll ask the horse to look at you, but he won't do it within the two-second limit. So you'll ask him to move his feet. One of the times that this happens, you'll find he stops with his feet farther from the fence — and closer to you — than previously. That's the first step in getting him to come to you on cue.

❶ This horse stopped facing the fence. John walked to where he could kiss to him and get the horse to look at him with even one of his eyes.

❷ John asks the horse to look at him with both eyes. You can see that if he looks (bending his neck) for long, his neck will tire.

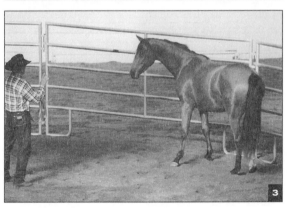

❸ Which is what happened. He moved his feet toward John.

❹ *Now the horse is parallel to the fence, and John steps to the right, again asking the horse to look at him with both of his eyes.*

❺ *Not only has the horse moved his feet off the rail, but he is stepping toward John.*

This is the same lesson you would use to teach a horse to be caught in a stall or pasture.

We don't want the horse to turn abruptly. Ideally, he'll turn his eyes to you, bend his neck, then relax his neck and finally move his feet. (Scared horses keep tension in their necks.) **The goal is first that the horse look at you with both eyes, then relax his neck, then move his feet.** So don't step so far behind the horse that he feels forced to move his feet before his neck relaxes, or ask him to look at you for too long for the same reason. **Each time you feel he's looked long enough, step back out in front of the horse, releasing him from bending his neck,** ideally without his diverting his gaze from you.

As you continue working in this pattern, and stepping farther into the middle of the pen, the horse will eventually turn so his shoulders are square to you, just like you would have moved your chair to face the TV. When he does, relax your posture, perhaps even walking away from him to let him know he did what you wanted.

Once you have that step down pat, you can have a little fun, stepping left and right, asking the horse's eyes to follow you. The horse may walk up to you, which is fine. Just remember to continue developing the cue to get his eyes, neck and feet to follow. If he walks up to you, consider that a sign that he is developing trust in you, but it was a choice the horse made — you were not in control.

Continue moving right. By this time, the horse has probably come off the rail. He may even be in the middle of the pen with you walking around him, his eyes locked on you (**horses love this step — they call it "lungeing the trainer."**). Even though he's now off the rail, the same rules apply. He should look at you. If not, kiss to him. If he doesn't look at you with both eyes within two seconds, tell his feet to get moving.

You can stop the lesson at any point; but, if you stop, leave the round pen. If you just hang around in there, without asking anything specific of him, the horse may get confused.

Getting both sides to respond

We began the lesson with the horse going to the left, which means that his left side is closest to us. But, won't always work from the left, so we'll have to train our horse to accept us on the right side as well. You'll find that the horse will try to position himself so that you are always on one side. You'll have to work through this tendency. For example, when you asked the horse to turn, you practiced inside and outside turns. **Unless you had insisted on both turns from both directions, the horse would have developed a habit of turning keeping you, say, in view with his left eye.**

While the horse is in the middle of the arena, and we are out in front of him, we'll do the step-right-step-left routine as before. But this time we'll step slightly left of his nose and call his eyes to us. If he responded correctly, good. If he didn't look at us, we should make his feet move. What he will most likely do is walk away from us, then turn to face us, with his left eye again closer than the right.

Again we'll go through the same step-left exercise. Most probably, the horse will not follow us with his eyes, and again we'll have to make him move. This time it may require sending him out to the fence and asking him to go right.

Chances are, he's going to want to go left, as before. He's comfortable now with us on his left, so he's likely to keep trying to change direction. We'll work with him, asking for turns just as we did in the earliest part of the round-pen training, until we have him going right consistently.

Then, we'll repeat the lesson on his other side, taking lots of time to get a good bend in the neck. **If we don't do that, and we allow the horse to tell us where he wants us to stand, who's in control?**

Moving forward

Remember, we said that looking at us with both eyes is a forward-motion exercise and that if the horse thinks, "back," you should ask him to step forward. **Continue doing the dance on the left and right until the horse's eyes follow you wherever you go.**

As the horse stands looking at you, walk up to him, then turn around and walk away. At this stage, we want the horse to feel comfortable with us walking up to him and eventually running up to him waving stuff, like saddle blankets. As in most lessons, this will take lots of repetitions. As you increase the pressure, by increasing your speed or "scariness," you'll see the horse's head go up, then relax. When you can approach the horse with a certain degree of "scariness" and he doesn't raise his head, then you are ready for the next step. Not only are you training for physical response, you are teaching the horse emotional control.

You want to get to a point where it seems the horse is "lungeing the trainer," that is, that the horse follows you with his eyes (and eventually his feet) wherever you go in the ring.

Following

After doing this a number of times, about 60 percent of horses will just walk behind you as if you were leading them. So, what about the other 40 percent?

We use the rule: **"First get the feet to move, then get them to move consistently, then in the direction you want."**

Step to the side and the horse will turn to face you as he's done before — his feet are moving. Now you want to get them moving every time you step away from him. So, step away such that he has to take a step forward. By working with this, you'll have the horse following you in no time.

Come when I call

But what if there's distance between you and the horse? Send him to the fence and get his feet walking left. Kiss to him and ask for the beginning of an inside turn. When the horse looks at you and begins to come to the inside, stop moving. The horse will stop. Walk up to him (pet him if you've done so in the past), then walk back to the middle of the pen. **If he tries to follow, tell him to wait, using ordinary traffic-cop body language.** (Can you see how this is also the beginning of teaching the horse to stand ground-tied?)

Again ask him to move left. Move across the pen and ask him for half an inside turn. As before, pet him and walk away. Repeat the exercise. You'll find instead of the horse travelling along the round-pen fence, he'll begin to travel in a circle smaller than the pen, and he'll be looking at you.

Continuing the lesson, as the horse comes to the inside, step to the right, asking him to continue moving (kiss and cue the hip). Your goal at this point is to get him to take a few steps toward you before he stops his feet.

If he stops, kiss to him. **If he doesn't move toward you within two seconds, move him out toward the fence and begin the exercise again.** What you'll find is that the horse's line of approach will be curved, not straight. Over time and repetition, he'll come toward you more directly.

Keep in mind that you are cueing specific parts of the horse — his nose and hip particularly. If he gets it right a few times, he just stumbled into it. It's your consistent rewarding of his getting it right that will enable him to truly learn the lesson. ▣

5

Sacking Out:
Not Just For Greenies

Sacking out, like giving to the bit,
is often misunderstood. We'll teach you how to train
your horse to cope with all kinds of scary stuff.

"Sacking out" is one of those terms, like "giving to the bit," that has different meanings to different people. To us, "sacking out" means systematically exposing our horse to lots of things approaching and touching him; however, we'll do everything in such a way that he won't get frightened enough to feel the need to react or flee.

Ironically, while we most often think of this exercise as preparation for a horse's first saddling, **the fact is that most experienced riding horses have never been sacked out properly. As a result, they sometimes get scared when something touches them unexpectedly, like a tall weed on their legs or a rider's raincoat.** Then, in their fright, they kick or buck, trying to get rid of the scary thing, and someone often gets hurt.

In the traditional sacking-out method, the horse is physically restrained, then his emotions are basically overloaded. Since he learns that he can live through the trauma, he won't be scared — theoretically — the next time he's faced with the same situation. In some cases it may work, but it's simply not worth the risk of injury or further scare.

For instance, if you were afraid of snakes, and we decided to sack you out the traditional way, we'd tie you in a chair, then bring out a large, but harmless snake, and we'd wave it around, putting it in your face, on your arms and so forth until we finally dropped it in your lap. How do you think you'd feel about all that? Probably the same

Frequently, the horse who pulls back on the lead rope or when he's tied is also headshy. That horse has two lessons to learn — "give to pressure" and overcoming headshyness.

way your horse feels if he's sacked out the traditional way. You'd live through it, and maybe in time you'd even be OK about it, but you'd have gone through unnecessary trauma first. Or maybe you'd live through it, but never get over the experience.

The concept behind traditional sacking out is desensitization — exposing the horse to various things until he's no longer scared of those particular things. If you could expose a horse to everything he'd ever experience, then that version of sacking out would be OK. **But, we can't anticipate every scare that a horse may get in his life, any more than we can anticipate what may frighten us.**

So, rather than just desensitize our horse, we must teach him a coping mechanism, a way to deal with his fears, whatever they may be and whenever they may spring up. The system I use establishes a way to train a horse's emotions, which is what keeps us both safe in a crisis.

Conditioned response

Imagine yourself walking down a dark street late at night. You hear footsteps quickly coming up behind you. Your heart rate increases; you start looking for a way to escape. Then, a sweet little girl's voice asks you what time it is. You answer her. She thanks you, and she leaves. Your blood pressure returns to normal. One minute later, you hear footsteps approach again. This time you don't get as scared.

Same question, same retreat. If this happens 10 times, aside from thinking the girl pesty, you aren't scared anymore. You've learned that the threat isn't big and it doesn't last long.

When we work with our horse, we will expose him to a threat so low that his blood pressure goes up, but then we will withdraw the threat early enough that he doesn't feel he has to escape.

Into the round pen

Let's assume our horse has been trained to go left and right, make inside and outside turns at specific locations, to stop parallel to the fence and to look at us with both his eyes. Now, with the horse stopped and looking at us, we'll begin the sacking-out process. **It's important that we don't tie the horse while we do this work. We must give the horse the option to move, because we want him to consciously choose to not move away.**

First we'll walk toward the horse in a calm, casual manner, not with an "I'm going to get you" approach. **Then, before he turns away from us, we'll turn away from him, indicating that all we wanted to do was approach him.** The first time we approach him, he doesn't know if we plan to eat him for lunch, clip his ears or just say hello. By walking away, we tell him our intention was not to cause him fear.

As we approach the horse, if he moves away or thinks "back up," we'll use our kiss and lariat to tell him to look at us. If he doesn't within two seconds, we'll ask him to move.

Let's assume that when we're 15 feet away from the horse he's fine, but at 14 feet he begins to pull his head away. We then know that we'll work within that one-foot distance for a while. We'll approach at 15 feet, then walk away. Then we'll approach at 14 feet 9 inches, then walk away and so forth. We'll do this until we can walk confidently up to 14 feet without his reacting.

Each time we walk away from the horse, we should follow a slightly different path. This does two things. It encourages the horse to move and relax between approaches, and it teaches the horse we can approach from more than one direction. If your horse isn't moving from time to time but appears frozen in place, he may have "locked up." Rather than his feeling OK about your approach, he's so scared that he feels he can't move, which is really dangerous. When he does move, it will be explosively. If you think your horse may have locked up, go back to the initial round-pen work, getting his feet to move.

John is touching the horse for the first time in this round-pen work. He pets the horse's forehead — the farthest point from her back feet.

Having stroked the horse's head, he walks away, ending a "mini-lesson." At this point it doesn't matter if the horse follows John or not. After a few steps John will walk back to the horse again and repeat the stroking.

As you work, one of the times you approach close to your horse and turn away, your horse is likely to follow you. This is a good sign; he's beginning to trust you.

Once you can get within 14 feet of the horse and have him comfortable, then work on 13, then 12 and so forth, each time walking away when the horse has done what you want — when he stands there looking at you.

If he takes his eyes off you, or begins to lean like he's going to move away, step away from him, kiss to him or wave your lariat — whatever you did before to tell him to look at you with both eyes and perhaps step forward.

Sometimes it seems you get stuck when working with your horse; perhaps you can only advance so far before he pulls away. If this happens a few times, back up in the lesson to a point where you are in control. **Remember that you should always work from a position of control. So, if you are unable to proceed in this lesson, return to asking for something that the horse will do 100 percent of the time.** Then build steps back to the lesson. This may mean, for instance, going back in the round-pen work to ask for direction changes.

The first touch

If we assume that the back feet are dangerous to touch at this stage, then we look for the least dangerous spot. Obviously, the horse's head comes to mind. One time, when you are standing slightly off to the side of the horse with him looking at you, pet him on the forehead between his eyes. Give him just a quick stroke, then walk away. If the horse pulls his head away, ask him to look at you with both eyes, as before. **Any time the horse is thinking about an escape plan, change his thinking by asking him to look toward you.**

Follow the same pattern that you did when approaching him: Pet him once, then walk away, pet two or three times, then walk away, etc. **Walking away is as important as petting: It tells him that he did what you wanted.**

Training principles

Sacking out, like round-pen work, is really a training principle, not just an exercise.

*Horses operate on a "run first, ask questions later" line of thinking. But, with this exercise, our horse learns he can wait and see what's happening before reacting. **When the horse doesn't react by moving away, and we then remove the threat, we reward his thinking.** Conversely, if we remove the threat while he's moving away, we end up teaching him to move when he perceives a threat. So for instance, if when we try to pet the horse and we take our hand down as he pulls his head away, he learns pulling away is effective.*

Horses quickly learn our patterns of behavior. That's part of why it's so important to take this lesson in small steps. You want to establish the right pattern. Once the horse moves away, you've lost the opportunity to sack him out. You can do something else to re-establish control (like call his eyes back to you or ask him to make an outside turn, then an inside turn), but then you have to change focus to return to what you were working on. This may happen several times as you work through sacking out your horse.

Fast hands

The slower you move your hands on your horse, the harder it is for him to stand still at this stage. If your horse is afraid of you touching his ears, it is easier for him to accept your hand sliding quickly over his ears than holding his ear for 30 seconds.

So, when you first pet a spot on your horse's head, run your hand over it quickly, then immediately withdraw your hand. The next time you can slow your hand slightly, next time a little slower and so forth until you can allow your hand to rest a split second. **A horse does not want to throw his head. So, if he pulls away from your hand, he's telling you he's afraid you may hurt him.** If your horse pulls away, backtrack in the lesson.

But, what if he lets you get up to him, but pulls his head away each time you reach toward his face? **Don't "chase" his head with your hand.** Do the same as with any other lesson — break it down into smaller pieces. Will the horse let you raise your hand close to your body without him pulling away? If yes, begin there. Raise your hand, then kiss to him to ask him to face you (your hand) with both eyes. When he does, take your hand down. Build from there until you can pet him.

We take whatever performance the horse gives us, then work to improve it. We can't expect the first few steps of a lesson plan to get us quickly to the goal. But, if we're thorough in the beginning, the later lessons move right along. Set little goals as you go through this lesson, touching the horse's ears, for instance, without him moving his head away.

Don't be discouraged if it seems to take a lot of time for the horse to be comfortable with you handling his head. The more fear a horse has, the longer it will take. Do not proceed with the lesson until he's comfortable with you petting his head.

On to the body

Now that we can pet the horse all over his head and ears, we will use the same principle to pet his whole body. Pet the head, then walk away. Approach the horse again, slightly to one side, pet his head, then allow your hand to run quickly past his ears onto his neck. Then walk away. Then approach from a slightly different position, calling the horse's eyes to you. Pet again, walk away and so forth. After a few times, the horse will be turning turn to face you.

Continue approaching, petting from the nose back onto the neck, then the shoulders, then the back and so forth, then walking away. **As before, if you feel the horse thinking about moving, withdraw your hand before he moves and ask him to look at you with both eyes, and perhaps to step forward.**

Pet the horse using different strokes and intensities. **Treat each body part as a separate lesson step.** Horses will often surprise you and react as you pet one place, when they didn't seem to even notice you petting somewhere else. As you work your way back on the horse, be sure to stand in a safe position as far forward as you can. If the horse begins to turn his hindquarters to you or threaten to kick, call his eyes (front end) to you.

Using this same technique, stroke the horse's legs, going part way down quickly, then removing your hand, then slowing your hand down and so forth, each time walking away.

As you get back to the hip, you will vary the exercise slightly. Approach from the front or side, pet from the front to back by the hip, then ask the horse to turn to you, then walk away.

WALKING AWAY IS AS IMPORTANT AS PETTING THE HORSE.

When the horse is comfortable with you approaching him from both sides and petting any part of his body, congratulate yourself. You have just sacked him out with your hand. Now we'll add something scarier than your hand.

What would be a little scarier than your hand, but not as scary as a tarp or saddle? Probably the lariat that has been in the arena with you all the time. **So start the whole sacking-out process again, using the lariat in place of your hand.**

While the horse may look at the coiled lariat strangely at first, that will give you a good chance to call his eyes and attention forward even when he thinks maybe he should back up. Start out, as before, petting his head with the lariat, then moving it over his ears, under his chin and down his neck, each time walking away after a stroke or two.

John gets the horse used to having his head handled, then getting it petted with the rope.

When he thinks the horse is comfortable enough with the coiled lariat, he leaves it on the horse's head. John immediately steps away, in case the horse get scared and makes a big move.

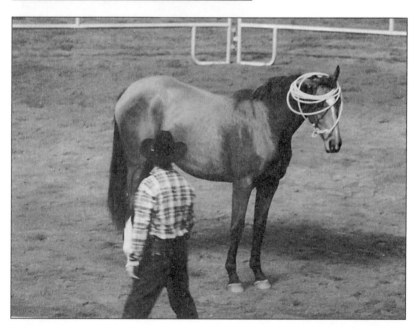

It is really important that the horse not only be comfortable with the rope all over his head, neck and hindquarters, but under his belly as well.

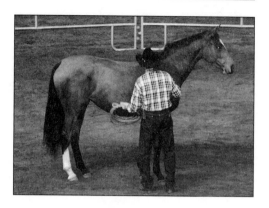

Wearing a hat

OK, it may not be the height of fashion, but teaching your horse to wear a lariat hat may make all the difference when riding through some low trees. We want our horse to be comfortable with things not only approaching him, but also resting on him, and even falling off him.

After the horse is comfortable with the lariat all over his head, just nonchalantly leave it on the top of his head and immediately walk away. Sometimes a horse will drop his head, and the rope will fall. When that happens, immediately kiss to the horse, asking him to look at you. If he spooked when the rope fell off, it's all the more important to kiss to him and ask him to face you. Pick up the rope, coil it up again, and repeat the exercise.

When the horse is comfortable with the lariat everywhere on his body — and we mean everywhere, even under his belly and up and down his legs — then you are ready to move onto the next prop.

What would be potentially scarier than the lariat, but less scary than the saddle blanket? Use your imagination. It may be a burlap sack or a towel. When he's solid with those, try a crinkly plastic bag, or how about something novel like a grooming brush? The object you use is less important than keeping the pattern the same — always training him to look toward you.

On toward saddling

Now, if your objective is to work up to saddling the horse, you'll next approach with a saddle blanket folded up about the same size as the coiled lariat. Again, pet the horse's nose with it, and walk

John pets the horse with a folded blanket as he did with his hand and coiled lariat. Note the position of the horse's head. He's telling John that he's still scared of that blanket in John's hand.

He doesn't like it under his belly, either. John continues to work with him, stroking him then walking away so he doesn't feel trapped.

When the horse accepts the folded blanket, John opens it and walks toward him with it fully open. He never opens it while standing near the horse.

away. Repeat the entire sacking-out exercise as before, eventually rubbing the horse all over and walking away. Each time, make sure the horse follows you at least with his eyes.

When your horse is comfortable with a folded saddle blanket, walk away from him, unfold the blanket about half-way and approach him with the open blanket. I don't unfold the blanket while I'm standing next to the horse, because then I'd miss the opportunity of approaching him with the larger item.

Work through unfolding the blanket until you can approach him with a blanket flapping, eventually dragging the blanket over his head and neck.

Traditional vs. Lyons method

Traditional Method:	Lyons Method:
■ Horse stands tied, often snubbed to a stout post.	■ Horse is free to stand still or move away.
■ No reward for the horse — he can only endure until its over.	■ He is rewarded at each step.
■ Great risk of injury to horse's neck or other parts as he struggles.	■ No risk of injury to the horse.
■ Risk of injury to the handler.	■ No risk of injury to the handler.
■ Can't stop until the horse settles down — then he's sweaty, frightened, and defeated.	■ Can stop anywhere along the program — the horse builds confidence.
■ Horse is excited at the end.	■ Horse is calmer at the end.
■ Trust is lost between the horse and the handler.	■ Trust built between the horse and the handler.
■ Must be done by an experienced trainer.	■ Can be done by a novice horseman.
■ Horse will be apprehensive of next lesson.	■ Horse will look forward to the next lesson.
■ Horse has learned to become excited and fearful.	■ Horse is learning to control his emotions.
■ Horse learns only to tolerate rather than accept new things. Has a defensive attitude.	■ Horse calmly accepts new things as part of his normal world. Has a relaxed attitude.

While there are many methods of sacking out a horse, some very systematic, gentle, and successful, the term "sacking out" generally has some pretty strong negative connotations. One usually pictures a frightened horse snubbed short to a post, struggling to avoid being hit by an object like a saddle pad. Usually, the horse is not hit hard enough to cause physical pain, the idea being to flood him with sensation. He ultimately overcomes his fear and figures out he isn't being hurt by the pad. The problem is that often the horse hurts himself, and sometimes the handler as well, as he struggles. ■PH

6

First-Saddling Essentials

*In addition to basic round-pen work and sacking out,
teaching this lesson can make you
and your horse feel both safe and confident
the first time you climb onto his back.*

Putting the saddle on for the first time could be a really big deal. Then again, your horse might take it in stride. Regardless of how well you've prepared him, some horses will buck a bit with the saddle on, and some horses, no matter how ill-prepared, won't. But, beyond the first buck or two, you don't want him to get a big scare. This lesson will help assure that a first saddling is a positive experience for you and your horse, and that he's ready to go to work when you step aboard.

First, the prerequisites

■ We've worked our horse in the round pen, teaching him inside and outside turns on cue at specific locations. We have established control — we've taught our horse that we can control his movement in a way that is safe for both of us.

■ We've taught him to turn and face us, and to look at us with both eyes when we are in the pen with him. That keeps us safely away from his back feet.

■ We've thoroughly sacked out our horse with our hand, then the lariat, then the folded and unfolded saddle blanket. We've set up a pattern that our intentions are trustworthy, even when we approach while carrying something unfamiliar. **It also sets up a pattern of him calming down after getting worried.**

Time spent thoroughly sacking out a horse is never wasted. The more comfortable he is with stuff all over his body, and particularly around his head, the safer we'll be when we start to ride.

After each thing we did with our horse, we walked away. Why is walking away so important? It tells the horse, "That's all I wanted." **The repetitions build confidence and establish the habit of him standing still as we approach from different angles and carrying all sorts of things.** In a few moments, we will approach him with a saddle, so we want him super comfortable with our approach.

To prepare the horse for saddling, we'll increase the potential scariness of the blanket by draping it over his back, then taking it off and walking away as before. We'll approach again, blanket open, and flap it up onto his neck, under his belly, around his neck, down around his legs, over his head and so forth — one motion at a time — petting the horse, then stepping away from him. **Each time, we'll walk away before the horse moves.**

If the horse should react to some of this, just keep your cool and ask him to look at you with both eyes. It's not uncommon for the horse to be uncomfortable with one part of this training. That does not mean he's being difficult; it's an opportunity to get him solidly cooperating with you and to tell him that when he's scared, you will not overwhelm him, but will deal with him in a confidence-building manner. Walk up to him, pet him and resume the lesson, perhaps lowering the threat slightly, and build up again.

This horse didn't mind being petted with the lariat, but he's definitely cinchy. He doesn't want any part of John petting his belly. Note in the first photo, John is approaching him, having walked away after petting his cinch area. His ears are back.

In the second and third photos, the horse attempts to bite the irritation. Notice that the horse tries different options, first to the side, then between his front legs. This horse was friendly and affectionate earlier in the lesson. But the horse let him know when John tried something he didn't like.

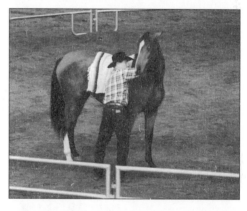

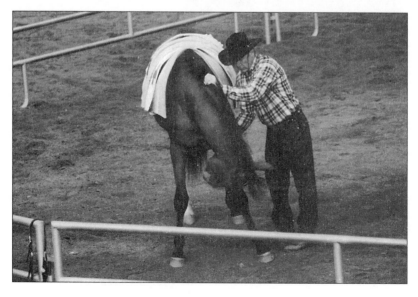

When we walk away, we want the horse to move a few steps, perhaps even to follow us. In fact, if he doesn't move, he may be "locked up," afraid to move, which is dangerous. **If your horse doesn't move on his own or turn to face you as you walk away, then you should ask him to move — while you are away from him. The fact that he's locked up will tell you he's not ready for more advanced work, but still has fear to deal with.** Go back to basic round-pen work.

If he reacted at any point, like when we had the blanket down around his legs (say, by kicking out at the blanket), we can assume that, should we fall off him and our head get down around his legs, he'll kick that, too. Not a risk worth taking! The horse's actions will tell us when he's ready for the next step.

If he gives us signs of anger or frustration (like stamping a foot), that, too, will tell us he is not ready to move onto saddling. Better to backtrack and get him solid in his training — and your control — than to risk a wreck.

So now, he stands like a trooper, barely raising his head as we do lots of dorky things with the saddle blanket, like making it into a shawl, plopping it in place on his back and patting his back pretty vigorously — one or two pats at a time. He doesn't care that we approach sometimes in a hurry and sometimes slowly, or sometimes from the left and sometimes the right. We can now approach him carrying stuff like he's been a riding horse for years and years.

Getting past cinchy

In the course of sacking out, you've probably hugged your horse a few times. Well, now we'll do that on a more intentional basis. With the blanket on the horse, give him a quick bear hug over his back with your hands down his both sides, and under his belly in the girth area, **making sure to stand forward by his shoulder, lest he cowkick**. Just a quick hug, and release before he has any reaction, then walk away. Gradually increase the duration of your hugs, each time releasing before the horse seems to want to move.

If the horse does react to your hugs, then first be sure you protect yourself from his attempts to bite or kick. Second, **make your hugs very quick — like a fly landing and leaving**. Just as it was easier for the horse to accept your hand moving quickly over his body when we were sacking him out, it will be easier for him if you put pressure on him, then release before he has a chance to react.

Don't be discouraged if everything went along fine until now. Just patiently work through the horse's objections, dropping back to

When we begin to saddle the horse for the first time, we don't make a big deal about it. Keeping a distance from people or fences, John places the saddle on the right side of the horse, with the left stirrup up on the horn.

The horse investigates the saddle. John notes his interest but matter-of-factly continues saddling him.

earlier steps, like asking him to move left and right and sacking out.

Then, with the horse wearing a saddle blanket, bounce a coiled lariat all around his body — not hard enough to make him to move, but enough that he realizes a little bumping-around is part of normal life. **Each time, quit bumping and walk away before the horse feels a need to move.**

Bring on the saddle

Now we step outside the round pen, pick up our saddle, cinch and saddle pad, and carry them to the middle of the pen. We are alone with our horse, as we've been through all the round-pen work — we don't want someone to hold the horse as we saddle him. And, we don't want to saddle our horse near the fence — we need plenty of room to get away from each other, should either of us get scared.

By the way, there's nothing wrong with being afraid. Even though **I've worked with thousands of horses, I am extra careful and have a healthy fear of them**. Even with good precautions and experience, it's still possible to get hurt.

As soon as the cinch is tight, step away from the horse on about a 45-degree angle to the front. His first step may be a big one.

Getting him dressed

First we'll put the saddle blanket on the horse, as we've done lots of times. Next, we'll put the left stirrup on the saddle horn and the latigo strap up on the seat. We'll approach the horse and put the saddle down nice and easy from the right, making sure all the straps (back cinch, stirrups, etc.) are hanging. If we put the saddle on from the left, we'd have to fuss with dropping the cinch, back cinch and so forth down on the right side and risk startling the horse.

If we've done all the work thoroughly up to now, the saddle won't be a big thing to the horse. Don't bring it to him saying, "Scary stuff. You'd better have a sniff or a good look." **Just assume the saddle is the next logical step, and put it quietly on his back.**

Walk around the front (but not under the neck) of the horse so you can cinch the saddle. If the horse walks off at this point, don't panic. Just kiss to him and ask him to turn to face you (that's part of why we did all that both-eyes work). **In all probability, the saddle won't have gone anywhere and the horse won't think anything of it.**

If you use a breastcollar, put that on next. I put the breastcollar on, then the back cinch, then the cinch, because I don't want anything hanging down while I cinch up the horse. If we've done all the preliminary work right, the horse won't move.

Then, standing by the horse's shoulder, lift the cinch ring and thread the latigo through it. Moving quickly, but not rushing, cinch the horse with a latigo knot, making the cinch as tight as you would if you were planning to ride. I prefer a latigo knot, rather than a cinch buckle, because, if the horse starts to move off before the buckle is tightened, the saddle could end up under the horse and scare him.

No matter what is left lying on the ground, you do not want to pick it up now. **Do not bend down or step in front of the horse for any reason. Also, this is the one time you do not want your horse to follow you. When he realizes the saddle is attached to him, his first step could be a big one.** Immediately step away from the horse, off to the side at about a 45-degree angle, watching him the whole time, and shoo him away from you.

At this stage, 50 percent of the horses buck, and 50 percent do not. If your horse bucks like crazy with the saddle, that does not mean he will buck with you on board. If he trots off like he's had the saddle on his whole life, don't become overconfident. That does not mean he is not going to buck with you on. What horses do at this stage doesn't tell us what will happen when we ride.

Never underestimate the importance of walking away. It breaks a lesson down into mini-lessons, reassuring the horse that he did what you wanted. It also gives you the opportunity to approach your horse again.

Never ever take your eyes off your horse while you are going through this training. Even though John is working with the stirrup, safety requires that he focus on the horse. He is slapping the stirrup against the saddle, not against the horse.

If the horse doesn't buck, don't encourage him to buck. There is nothing he needs to "get out of his system," and you do not want to teach him to buck.

Begin to ask the horse to work in the pen, taking his mind off the saddle and re-establishing order and control. Don't let him come right up to you at first, but instead work on walking, trotting and making turns, as you did early on. Then ask the horse to stop and face you. Walk up and pet him. He may follow you as before, which is OK.

Sacking again

Begin the sacking out process all over, this time with the saddle on. Your horse's excitement level is likely to be higher than when you left off, so you'll do easy stuff first, like with the lariat — petting him with it and walking away.

In addition to sacking him out with the lariat and another saddle blanket, slap the stirrups against the saddle (not against the horse). Pat the saddle, make noise, wiggle the saddle around and so forth. At this point, use your imagination to accustom the horse to as much as you can before you put your foot in the saddle. Each time, though, remember to walk away or stop making noise before the horse feels the need to move. By now, the horse should follow you as you walk away.

Second and third saddling

Some notes about what you might expect the next few days you work with the horse: If the horse bucked the first day, he's likely to buck with the saddle the second day. Even if he didn't buck the first day, he may on the second. Don't do anything about it on the second day, but note it mentally.

The third day saddling, if the horse bucked the first two days, put a halter and lariat or lunge line on the horse. If he moves off and begins to buck, turn his head toward you with a quick pull. You do not want him to get in the habit of bucking or, worse yet, to think that's what you want him to do. Immediately give him another job, and the bucking will go away on its own. That said, **the more you can do the first day to get him comfortable with the saddle, the less the chance he'll buck on the second.**

Clinicians and trainers often feel under pressure to produce results quickly. I used to see how quickly I could take an unbroken horse and get safely in the saddle. But I don't do that anymore. In fact, on horses that I start at home, I do lots of ground exercises before I ever get on the horse. That not only makes riding much safer, but it actually makes learning easier for the horse.

John attaches a rope to the saddle horn. It will let him put pressure on the saddle and accustom the horse to a new sensation.

Gradually allow slack in the rope and, as the horse feels comfortable, move around with it. Don't chase the horse with the rope. If the horse begins to get upset, kiss to him and ask him to turn to face you.

Taming dragons

The next thing I do is eliminate the fear of dragons chasing the horse. I'm sure you've seen a dragon chase a horse, perhaps even into a fence. **A loose lead rope or lunge line trailing behind the horse was chasing him — hence, the draggin' lead.**

However, we certainly don't need dragons interfering with our ride, so we'll take care of that before we get on. We'll start by looping one end of the lariat over the saddle horn and asking the horse to walk in the round pen to the left. At first we'll walk about 10 feet from him, preventing the rope from bumping him or dragging. We don't want to scare the horse; instead, we'll continue the same sacking-out philosophy we've been using.

From time to time, I'll give a little tug on the rope. Generally, if the horse is relaxed, he'll turn to face me. Then I'll walk up and pet him, then ask him to walk again.

As time goes on and the horse is comfortable with the first step, allow more slack in the rope, eventually letting it drag a bit. Then work your way back so you can walk behind the horse with the rope touching his flank. Ask him to face you, then walk up and pet him with the rope.

When he's comfortable with all that, work up to flipping the rope in the air. Follow the same pattern, making sure that the horse is comfortable with the rope moving around him, including around his legs and under his belly. **Don't hit him with the rope as if you want him move, but bump him just enough to let him know that if something like a rope bumps him from time to time, it's nothing to get scared about.** Like everything we do with the horse, we'll work this exercise from both sides, and then we'll be nearly ready to mount up. ▣

7

Spook In Place

You can't expect your horse to never get scared,
but you can teach him how to deal with his fears.
In fact, you have a responsibility to do so.

W e've all experienced it. A pleasant trail ride chatting
with friends as we ride along, reins relaxed, when suddenly — out of nowhere — a deer bounds across the
trail. Both you and your horse are startled. Whether
your horse responds with a momentary bug-eyed snort or an out-of
control bolt depends on whether you've taught him to "spook in
place." With the spook-in-place exercise, he'll learn that it's okay to
"spook," as long as he doesn't move his feet.

Spooks are scary for both people and horses — and they should
be. Easily startled, horses instinctively run from dangers, both imagined and real. Riders become tense during a spook, because they
realize that the consequences — a bad fall, a wild crash into a fence,
or a leap into the path of an oncoming vehicle — can be deadly. A
horse who spooks a lot isn't safe, much less fun.

Just as we can't expect ourselves to never feel fear, we can't ask
our horse to never be afraid. However, we can teach him what to do
when he becomes afraid.

Scared, but not fleeing

Although we should certainly try to expose our horse to as many
equine-eating monsters as possible — like flags, plastic bags, news-
papers blowing across the ground, tarps draped over the fence —

Begin with a soft "boo," just enough to get his attention, but not big enough to scare the horse.

When the horse just stands there, walk to him and pet him. You are laying the foundation for the "spook in place" work. You want the horse to startle but not move his feet.

we simply can't sack out our horse with absolutely everything that may come his way or cross his path. So, we need to teach him what to do when he gets scared. We need to replace his natural instinct to flee with a conditioned response to stand and face the thing that scares him. We must teach him to spook in place.

Basically, this is sacking out for his emotions. Rather than teaching the horse not to fear specific objects, spooking in place teaches the horse what to do when something scares him. We'll let him know it's OK to be afraid, as long as he faces his fear without moving away.

One word of caution. Fear is a peculiar thing. One person may be afraid of flying, and another afraid of thunder. So, too, what one horse barely notices may send another running bug-eyed around the round pen. **It's easy to miscalculate your horse's reactions, so it's important that you've first mastered the basic round-pen work — that you have good control over your horse's movements.** Be sure that you have developed cues to tell your horse to make outside and inside turns, to stop and to come to you. If there's any doubt about your control of him when he's loose — any doubt he won't turn and face you on cue — then go back and repeat your round-pen training thoroughly before you proceed with this lesson.

Now, on to the lesson. You'll need no special equipment. You should, however, gather a collection of potentially spooky objects, ranging from a gum wrapper to a towel to a big tarp.

The lesson's most important ground rule is that, although you will deliberately scare your horse, none of the spooky objects will ever hit him.

Turn your horse loose in a confined area, like a round pen, and ask him to look at you. From across the pen, whisper "boo." Then turn and walk away. Chances are, your horse won't spook, but he'll wonder what you are up to.

WITH THE SPOOK-IN-PLACE EXERCISE, YOUR HORSE WILL LEARN THAT IT'S OKAY TO "SPOOK," AS LONG AS HE DOESN'T MOVE HIS FEET.

Next, turn toward your horse and say "boo" in a normal speaking voice. If your horse is still standing there, turn and walk away or walk up and pet him. After about three little boos, increase the tone in your voice to "Boo," working up to "BOO!" (OK, I know what you're thinking. You're saying to yourself, "I realize John always breaks down lessons into lots of easy little steps, but this is downright ridiculous." Have patience here. You're establishing an important pattern for your horse.)

When you make a scary sound and your horse stands still, walk up to him and praise him with plenty of petting. If he takes a couple of tentative steps away, which shows that he may be thinking about leaving, but doesn't actually flee, ask him to look at you and praise him for that, too. That indicates he changed his mind, which is great, because he's getting a handle on his emotions.

If, on the other hand, your horse actually moves away, ask him again to look at you. If he keeps moving, don't worry; you can use this to your advantage. Move him around the pen a few times, then

Even after all the sacking out, when John unfurls the saddle blanket, the horse decides to exit. John kisses to him, asking him to look at him (and the blanket).

This step is really important, because for the horse's whole life, he'll have people carrying things approaching him — from the farrier with his tool box, to the rider with a saddle, to the groomer with clippers, to the show official with a blue ribbon.

again ask him to turn to face you. (One note, if he's running scared and out of control, of course, don't encourage him to run. Safety is always the No. 1 concern.) Pay attention to your horse to interpret his degree of panic, emotion and growing calmness, so you can temper your actions accordingly.

If he figures out that, when you scare him, he can move around the pen and stop again, always "escaping" in the same direction, **then ask him to stop and make an inside turn, returning via the escape route**. If he runs off again and again, that will tell you two things. First, the scare was too big: back off to smaller "boos." Second, just as in initial round-pen training, he needs more motivation to stop and face you.

In that case, when he moves off around the round pen, keep him going a few laps, so he's not just in the pattern of once around, then stopping. These things may not happen at the low-threat "boo" stages, but sooner or later, as you increase the intensity of the scare, they will.

Remember, your goal is for him to stop and face you (eventually to face what is scaring him) when he's frightened. You don't want him to think that running around the pen willy-nilly is the right reaction.

Dealing with specific fears

If the horse is afraid of one thing in particular — say, a whip — we can teach him to no longer fear that one thing. In fact, if your horse is afraid of something fairly common, something he'll likely encounter often in the course of his life, it's our responsibility to help him conquer that fear. It's cruel to let him go through life afraid.

To help him overcome his fear, we'll use the standard sacking-out method. In short, we'll expose him to the scary object in such a low-threat manner that he doesn't react, or if he does react, he doesn't move his feet. We'll give you the basic concept here, but you'll have to work out the specifics to focus on what frightens your own horse.

Let's say that your horse isn't so scared of a whip that he bolts for the next county, but that, if you raise a whip while leading him, he throws his head up, stiffens his neck and looks for an escape route. In that case, you might start, from a distance away from him, by picking up the whip in a non-threatening manner. Then, before your horse gets anxious, put the whip down. The next time, pick it up, move forward six inches, then lay it down again. Keep working through that sequence — introduce a tiny threat, the horse doesn't move, so you remove the threat — until you can touch the horse with the whip.

Touch him gently with the whip, perhaps on his shoulder, for a few seconds. If you think that he'll move away in three seconds, remove the whip in two. Keep approaching him, touching and eventually stroking him, until the horse deems it "no big deal" when you pick up the whip and move it around or stroke him with it.

Let's say he didn't mind you having a whip, but he gets afraid when he sees someone else carrying a whip, or making whip noises. Develop an exercise following the same concept. Ask someone to walk by carrying a whip, close enough that the horse sees him but doesn't try to move away. Then ask the person to walk by again and again, each time adding a bit more movement to the whip, making sure the perceived threat isn't so large that the horse moves. If the horse moves out of fear, then the whip's movement was too big a threat for this stage of the lesson.

Depending on your horse, it may take 20 passes or 200 times of a person walking by in varying stages of whip-waving before the horse says, "Oh there's a person waving a whip around. Been there, done that. No big deal."

Make sure the horse is solid at one threat level before moving on to the next. At any point in the lesson, if the horse reacts to the threat by moving, don't scold him. He's not trying to be difficult. The perceived threat was simply more than his "nerves" would tolerate. Don't make the mistake of thinking, "Oh, good grief, horse. You should know this by now. You're just being silly." It does not matter if he's being "silly." What matters is that you remain calm and patiently work through the progression to teach him not to move his feet when he's frightened. Just be thorough and stick to the program.

Whether your horse is afraid of the whip, a saddle blanket, clippers, garbage cans or having his head handled, develop a lesson plan specific to dealing with those problems. Bottom line, whenever you know your horse has a specific fear, help him get over it. If you shrug it off and decide to "just live with it," sooner or later his fearful reaction will cause a wreck.

Increasing the "scare"

Once you and the horse grasp the basic idea with the little "boos," then you can add body language, eventually jumping toward him or flapping your arms like a chicken. As you do this, be sure not to use any motion or signal that you've used previously to tell the horse to move off. You don't want to "burn a cue," despooking him with that cue. You also don't want to use any body language that you want to hold specific meaning for him in the future.

For instance, if you plan to wave your arms and jump at him to tell him, "No, don't run into the barn" when he comes in from the pasture, don't de-spook him with that signal.

With the full range of "boos" completed, you should next increase the intensity of the scare. Try a scary sound, like a "raspberry." At the same time, ask him to turn in to you. As you continue this exercise, increase the pressure gradually — bump up your raspberry to a hoot, then to a shout, then with waving arms. **Each time, try to raise his blood pressure, so to speak, without overpowering his emotions and causing him to run.**

At each scare level, including when we will be working with props, you want a reaction from the horse — ideally a heads-up "flinch" as he's startled, but not a whirl-and-run or jump-to-the-side reaction. Make sure that you release the horse from the scare the moment he turns to look at what scared him.

When he doesn't startle at a particular "scare," then you are ready to increase the intensity of the pressure or stop the exercise. **Once the horse no longer "flinches," stop scaring him with that motion, sound or object. You don't want to harass the horse or go overboard with the exercise to the point that the horse becomes aggressive.** The same is true when sacking out, for instance, with clippers. It's one thing to accustom the horse to clipping; it's another thing to ask him to stand three hours with the clippers running just as an irritant.

Add props to the production

With the same concept in mind, and remembering the ground rule (no hitting the horse), it's time to bring in the spooky objects you gathered earlier. Start with the smallest object and work your way up. For instance, in addition to "booing," how about wrinkling a gum wrapper?

When he can handle that — by facing you and not moving away — graduate to something scarier, say a small plastic bag. Each time, of course, praise him profusely when he does the right thing.

Next, shake a towel or smack a saddle blanket against your leg. **Make sure the horse is solid at one scare before going on to the next.** Horses not only fear what they can see but they fear noises as well. As you incorporate noisy scares, such as you kicking a garbage can around, then your horse will learn to face the scary noise as well as the scary object. Use your imagination about what might be a little bit scarier than the last thing you use. Perhaps try rattling a can of rocks, banging a pail or garbage-can lid, swinging a rope or opening an umbrella.

It's unlikely that your horse will stand still through every scare. That's OK. When he moves away, realize you need to backtrack. Turn the pressure down until he can stand, facing the scary object, and proceed again from there.

You can increase the excitement level and thus teach your horse to control his emotions, which is what this is all about, by adapting this exercise. Once you have your horse de-spooked in the round pen, why not try him on a lunge line in the arena or out in a pasture (assuming you've taught him to lunge and yield to pressure on a rope)? The reason you put him on a lunge line when he's outside the round pen is so you can maintain control.

You'll find that what didn't scare him at all in the round pen, might over-scare him in the arena or pasture (haven't we all experienced this first-hand when riding?). So, make sure that your first scare or two outside the round pen is low-threat.

You can add extra steps to this lesson, working up to having the horse deal with very scary objects or situations, but I wouldn't do that with every horse. These basic low-threat exercises are good, but if a horse is pretty solid to begin with, you don't want to risk that he'll get really scared.

How much is too much?

How far you take the spook-in-place exercise depends on many factors. If you carry it too far, using extremely scary objects or noises, your horse might get really frightened, and then you'll have a bigger job on your hands to de-spook him.

If a horse gets really, really scared, his fear can last a long time, making him even spookier than before you started. (On the other hand, the more solid you get the horse with this work, the better he'll be in the long run, but getting there may be a really big project.)

If a horse is basically calm and seldom spooky, I would not do too much spook-in-place work, following the theory, "If it isn't broken, don't fix it." *But if you have a*

After the horse is very solid when you wave objects around, try tying a tarp to a rope, and toss it in the air. When he's OK with that, drag the tarp on the ground. Each step of this presents different challenges, so don't proceed too quickly or overscare your horse. Lots of petting is important, too.

spooky horse, for both his and your safety, you must deal with his fear, so teach him to spook in place.

So, how do you know if he's spooky or not? Well, it isn't hard to tell with some horses — some are calm no matter what goes on around them, and others are jumpy every time a leaf hits the ground. The horses in between are tougher to gauge.

If a horse reacts so strongly to normal scary things in his environment — when you drag a trash can down the driveway, for instance — that he risks being out of control, then do the spook-in-place work.

If it takes more than 10 or 15 minutes to put a winter blanket on him the first time, and it seems like he's truly terrified by the blanket, like he might jump on you if you move too fast, then he needs sacking-out lessons as well as spook-in-place.

If the horse's reaction puts either you or him in danger you should deal with his fear. PH

You can adapt this lesson to working under saddle — once the horse has learned to "spook in place" without a rider. Here Zip "spooks" at a tarp tied to a post, but he doesn't whirl away because he's been trained to face the scary thing.

8

First Ride

*This is the day many horseowners
have anxiously awaited — the day of the first ride.
What should you do to help assure it will be a great
experience for both you and your horse?*

Whether you've raised this horse yourself or bought him ready-to-start, by the time for his first ride, emotions — and expectations — are high. It's easy to get excited and miss an important step, so first the preliminaries, then into the saddle.

Your first objective is to get on and off your horse safely and without scaring him. If you meet your first objective and want to go on to other lessons, that's fine. But, keep your attention focused on what you are doing at that moment, not on what you'll do next or on what the future holds. Pick a day when neither you nor your horse will feel rushed or distracted. Allow enough time that the feed cart won't be rolling by at a critical moment.

Then, think about what you will wear. **You do not want to get on your horse with anything that can flap around or get caught on the saddle.** Tuck in your shirt; don't wear a jacket; save that big belt buckle for another ride. You'll want boots with a heel, not sneakers or shoes that could get hung up in a stirrup, and a helmet is always a good idea. **Know your lesson plan inside and out, so that you don't get confused, upset or make an impulsive decision.**

It's a good idea to make sure there is someone else at the barn, but not in the pen with you. You don't want anyone holding your horse when you get on.

By the time you are ready to teach this lesson, you should have already completed the basic round-pen work and thoroughly sacked

Step away from the horse immediately after tightening the cinch. It's not uncommon for a horse to buck with the saddle the first day or two. That does not necessarily mean he'll buck with a rider on him.

out your horse with a saddle pad (both folded and open) and a lariat. Ideally, you've taught your horse good leading manners and you've taught him to "spook in place." You've also made sure he's not the least bit headshy.

You've saddled your horse and turned him loose, moving him around the pen. He's comfortable moving around wearing a saddle and with ropes hanging off him and dangling down around his feet.

Even after all that, **ask yourself if there is anything else you can do to make your horse feel more comfortable and secure with you and his training.** Is there any lesson you might have done better, any indication of fear on the horse's part that you just dismissed? **If you're confident that you've done all the background work well, you can move forward.**

There are a million lessons you can teach your horse from the ground — everything from shaking his head "yes" and "no" to flying lead changes on the lead rope. **The better trained the horse is before you climb on board, the better it is for both of you.** It may be unrealistic to teach him all those lessons, but there is at least one more lesson you should work through before stepping into the saddle — you should "connect the rein to the hip."

The most powerful part of the horse, the muscular part that propels him forward is his hindquarter. Using the rein, teach your horse to step his hindquarters over to the side. Just take the slack out of one rein, beginning on the left side, and pull the rein toward his withers. Hold tension on the rein until he steps to the right with his hind feet. He can't bolt forward or buck very easily when he's stepping over. Not only that, in order to bolt or buck, he has to stiffen

Review all the prior lessons before getting on your horse for the first time. It will refresh the horse's memory and give you both confidence.

Here John works with the rope, throwing it over the horse's head to be sure he's not headshy. John won't get on a headshy horse.

his neck; it's difficult to do that when his head is turned to the side, as it will be with this exercise. You can use this as a safety valve when you go to step on your horse. **If you fear he may kick you, ask him to move his hindquarters to his right, away from you.**

Bridled and nearly ready

In order to "connect the rein to the hip," you need a rein, so the horse has to wear a bridle. **When it comes time to bridling him for the first time, I don't make a big deal about it.** Having already handled his head extensively, the horse doesn't mind if I put my finger gently between his lips. With the top of the bridle in my right hand,

Before proceeding to the next step in the lesson, John will approach the horse and tap all over the saddle, lift the stirrups and let them drop without hitting the horse, then pet the horse and walk away lots more times.

my left hand guides the bit between the horse's teeth. Once the horse opens his mouth, my right hand raises the bridle and pulls it back over the horse's ears, with my left hand assisting. **I don't believe that the horse needs time to get used to the bridle.** I just put it in his mouth, then proceed with the lesson.

You may have taken weeks to get to this point, or you may have only worked with your horse for a few days, but today when you go into the round pen, you'll want to go through a little review. Spend about 10 minutes going over basic round-pen work, asking the horse to move make inside and outside turns at specific locations. Go through the sacking-out process, making sure to walk away after each exposure. By walking away, you remind the horse that you are not going to trap him — that when he does what you want, you'll back off, giving him some space. **Saddle him, making sure to tighten the cinch, then step away from him right away, asking him to move off.**

Your goal is to review the lessons in the horse's mind, not tire him out. **You cannot get a horse tired enough that he can't buck, without also endangering his health. Actually, you want him to feel energetic — no student learns his best when he's worn out.**

Continue through the lessons you've taught him, including connecting the rein to the hip. When you feel that your horse is consistent in his responses to you, it's time to begin the new lesson. Incidentally, that's always when you'd want to start a new lesson

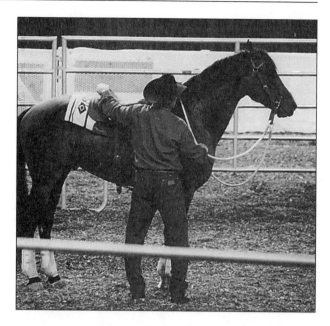

John checks to make sure the horse is comfortable with the saddle, wiggling it around and messing around with the stirrup. The horse is on alert, but accepts what John is doing.

with a horse. If the horse isn't doing familiar stuff well, then he'll have a hard time with new material, and you are more likely to get frustrated and become impatient.

So is all this preliminary stuff important? Yes. It's education and repetition, which gives you consistency, something you can count on every day — and today's an important day. Check your cinch, and you'll be ready to proceed.

Getting ready to mount

Approach the horse, as you've done a million times before when sacking him out. Pat the saddle and wiggle it around then walk away. Approach again, pick up the left stirrup and gently let it drop; then pet your horse's neck and walk away, ending another mini-lesson.

When the horse is comfortable with you thumping on the saddle, handling the stirrups, and wiggling everything around, then again (you knew that would be the next word) approach the left side of the horse. Take most of the slack out of the left rein, without allowing the right rein to hang so low the horse could step in it. Pet the horse, drop the left rein and walk away. **If the horse moves when you pick up the rein, repeat the exercise until you can approach and adjust the reins without the horse moving.** You want him to understand that you can adjust the reins without his having to move.

Never take your eyes off your horse when you are training him. You want to be able to quickly step away from him should it seem like he's going to bolt forward. Turn his head to you if you sense that he's about to kick.

Be sure to stand up by your horse's head so you are out of range should he decide to kick. (Of course, if he does attempt to kick, you can also use the rein to ask his hips to step to his right.) When you step away, be sure that you do so toward the front but not directly in the horse's path, so you can get out of range should he get scared and jump forward.

Approach again, adjust your reins, pick up the left stirrup, raise your left foot just to touch it, then put your foot back on the ground. Let go of the stirrup. Give your horse a big bear hug around the base of his neck, hanging heavily for a moment, then step away. Repeat this step until you know that the horse is comfortable with it.

Each time you step away, you let the horse know he did what you wanted, and you give him a moment to relax. He may drop his head and follow after you a step or two, which is OK. If he doesn't, ask him to move a step or two; don't give him the opportunity to "lock up." **If at any point the horse seems upset, just backtrack to an earlier step. Time spent here is well invested; don't hurry this process.**

Approach again, adjust reins, pick up the stirrup, and this time, add a little weight when you put your foot in the stirrup. Pet the horse, remove your foot, drop the rein and walk away. Continue this process, each time putting more weight on the stirrup and for longer

When standing in the stirrup, keep your center of balance over the middle of the horse. Keep your left hand on the saddle horn, so you can quickly push away and step down if necessary. Pet the horse with your right hand.

periods. You'll want to repeat this at least 25 times.

Now approach, adjust reins, step into the stirrup and hop, as a person might who was working up to getting on a tall horse. Then take your foot out of the stirrup, pet the horse and walk away. By the way, from time to time, it's a good idea to pet your horse all over, really make a fuss over him. You want to continue to be sure that he's comfortable with his head and whole body being handled.

This next time, approach, gather the rein, hold the mane, put your foot in the stirrup, grab the back of the saddle, then reverse the process and walk away. Repeat this sequence, working up to hopping in that position, then putting weight in the stirrup, holding the mane and back of the saddle. Stand close to the horse's shoulder to avoid putting undue stress on his withers or pulling him off balance.

Both sides now

You guessed it. Now that you have the easy side done, it's time to approach the tall side of the horse. At least, it always feels like the horse is taller on the right side than the left. Still, it's important to do both sides of the horse, not only because someday you may have to mount and dismount from the "wrong" side, but also because you want your horse to be comfortable with movement and handling on the right as well as the left.

Ready for lift-off

Now go back to the left side of the horse. This time, follow the same sequence as you've been doing, but when you're ready to get off the ground, grasp the mane and the back side of the saddle and spring off your right foot (the one that's been hopping a million hops). Go immediately all the way up, so that you are standing with your weight balanced over the saddle.

Don't creep up the horse's side or go up only halfway. You don't want to pull the saddle off balance, which would be uncomfortable and potentially scary for the horse. **Just go straight up, smoothly and quickly (not over, and not with your stomach on the saddle).** Move your left hand from the mane to the saddle horn, then step down and away from your horse, stepping toward his head as you've been practicing.

Breathe a big sigh of relief and begin again. Approach, gather reins, pick up stirrup, put your foot in the stirrup, left hand on the mane and right hand on the back of the saddle. **Step up to your full height, making sure that your weight is over the horse's center of gravity. Immediately move your left hand to the horn.** Pause for a moment, then dismount as before.

Don't forget to let your horse know how proud you are of him. Pet him often to reassure him, as you've been doing up until this part of the lesson.

When you've repeated the lift-off many times on the left, do the same thing on the right. When you and the horse are comfortable, you are ready for the next step.

Now lift off on the left as before. This time, keep your left hand on the horn, but begin petting the horse with your right hand. Before this part of the lesson is over, you'll want to have petted his neck, shoulders and hindquarters. Pay particular attention to petting the croup (halfway between the back of the saddle and the tail) where you may possibly bump him with your right foot when you finally swing aboard. Of course, you'll want to do lots of repetitions of this part of the lesson from both sides of your horse. **Don't move that left hand from the horn. You want to have an easy way to push away from the horse, should it be necessary.**

Before I get on a horse for the first time, I ask three questions:
1. Have I done everything I can to get this horse prepared for a rider on his back?
2. Do I think the horse is going to buck with me?
3. Do I think the horse is going to be just fine?

The answer to No. 1 is always, "no." There is always something else I can do. But by asking myself that question, I can review what I've done. It may be that I've missed something big. If so, I sure want to figure that out before I sit in the saddle. If I feel I've done everything reasonable, then I go on to question No. 2.

If the answer to No. 2 is, "yes," then I continue preparatory work — my horse is not ready to mount, yet.

When I can answer, "yes" to No. 3, then I'm ready to get on. But — not on this horse.

Ready to ride

In my own mind, the horse that I'm going to mount is not this unbroke horse — instead, it's the horse that I am most familiar with and most confident of. I don't ever get on a green horse as if he's a stick of dynamite about to explode. I get on him as if he's my old riding buddy — the one I can count on. **I pretend I'm getting on Zip.**

So, just like I get on Zip sometimes, I'll probably bump this unbroke horse with my leg as I swing on board. That's OK. **I don't want to train him to stand for a perfectly balanced rider, then step on board in my usual way one day and scare him. I'll let him know right from the beginning what he can expect.**

The time to decide that you are going to actually swing up into the saddle is when you are 10 feet away from the horse. Don't go through the bouncing lesson, each time wondering if this is the time, and then suddenly get brave and "go for it." Approach your horse as you've been practicing. Then:
■ Gather your rein.
■ Put your left hand on the mane.
■ Put your left foot in the stirrup.
■ Grab the back of the saddle with your right hand.
■ Bounce, on your right foot then stand up on the left stirrup and swing your right leg over the horse's back.
■ Sit down in the saddle, as you would normally (but do not put your right foot in the stirrup).
■ Immediately move your left hand from the mane to the horn.

- Immediately dismount and step away from your horse.
- Breathe a sigh of relief and go pet your horse. You and he have just completed your first ride.

Now, as you've no doubt guessed, you are going to repeat the getting-on process, each time sitting a moment longer in the saddle before dismounting. You are going to practice from both sides, even mixing it up — mount left, dismount right and so forth. Lots and lots of repetition, until he really feels like that familiar old trail horse.

What if he moves?

If he moves as you put your foot in the stirrup or begin to mount, turn his head toward you using the left rein. That will move the kicking end away. If he does move away, he's not ready for mounting yet, no matter how much preparation you think you've done.

If, after lots of preparatory work, the horse still moves as you begin to mount, go back to the directional control lesson — asking him to move left and right, back and forward — then giving him the opportunity to stand still. You don't want to do this as if you are punishing the horse or correcting bad behavior. You want to let your horse know that standing still is OK; that, in fact, it's what you want him to do.

So, if the horse steps forward, ask his hip to move to the side. Then give him the chance to stand. If he backs up, ask him to step forward. **Remember that from the early round-pen work, we want the horse to think "forward," not back.** Even if this takes quite a few tries, don't become discouraged. **Any time you are working on one thing, and the horse does something that requires you to work on something else, that something else becomes the new objective.** So, even though you were working on mounting, if the horse doesn't stand, you should forget about mounting, and concentrate on teaching the horse to stand.

At no time should you scold the horse. You will lose a lot of trust and create unwanted behaviors in the process. Be patient and change your objectives. You are planning to ride this horse for years. An extra few hours at the front end can pay big dividends later. On the other hand, if you rush now, you may create problems that take a long time to work through.

If the horse walks off once you are on him, don't panic. No doubt you've ridden a horse who walks around the round pen. What you don't want to do is scare your horse. Allow him to walk. **When you want him to stop walking, take the left rein (the one that is already**

Before a demonstration crowd, I worked this unbroke horse through the round-pen work, then sacking, saddling and mounting. I am riding him for the first time and have taken him outside the round pen. I didn't ask him to walk, but I'm not concerned that he's walking, because I can use my left rein to make his hips go right and thus stop his forward motion if necessary.

shortened) and ask his hips to step over. When they do, release the rein. If he walks again, ask again, until he stops his feet. Then pet the horse and dismount.

If the horse walks off during the first 15 or so times that you mount him, that may tell you he's not quite comfortable. Usually, those horses are also a bit uncomfortable with the dismounting process.

When you are ready to dismount, do so in one motion, being ready to use the rein to ask the horse's hips to step over if it seems that he's about to spook as you come back to the ground. If you've been in the saddle for a few minutes, the horse may have forgotten about your getting down, and he may become startled. If that's the case, practice mounting and dismounting until the horse no longer moves off or seems worried about any of your activities.

What if you think he's about to buck? Use the rein to ask his hips to step over. If he crow-hops, again use the left rein and ask his hips to step over. **When he stops, dismount, remembering that he may get frightened as you get off.** Then go back to basics.

This horse is putting his head down just to stretch his back and get accustomed to the feel of a rider. When a horse puts his head down, it does not necessarily mean that he's about to buck.

What's next?

So you have successfully gotten on and off your horse a bunch of times. What else should you do? Nothing. Don't kick him to get him moving, and don't try to steer much if he walks on his own. Just let him get used to you getting on and off and sitting up there. Keep your rein handy to connect to his hip if you need to control him, and enjoy your success.

In time, you'll go on to teach him to walk forward using a rein cue, not your seat, voice or legs.

In all probability, if you worked painstakingly through this lesson, your first ride was perfect. Your horse didn't rear, dive for grass, spook, bolt wildly or call to his friends. Your challenge will be to continue his training in the same way without teaching him any of those bad behaviors. ▨

Section II

Developing
Riding Cues
and
Solving Riding Problems

9

The "Don't Shy" Cue

Exit, stage left — or is it stage right?
One can't stop to ask on a horse who shies.
Ironically, there's no cue to say, "Don't shy."
So what are we to do?

You are riding along, minding your own business and enjoying the day, when suddenly your horse spies something scary, stiffens his body and prepares to make a quick getaway. All at once you may find yourself angry, frustrated and grabbing mane — that is, assuming you aren't left in the dust. But it doesn't have to be that way.

Anyone who has ever been on a shying horse knows that the horse is not under control. But it may have seemed he was under control just moments before the shy. What can we do to prevent another upset?

We use individual lessons or exercises to get our horse more responsive to specific requests. If he walks too slowly, we teach him the "speed up" cue. If he bolts from the trot into a gallop, we teach him canter departs. But, problems like shying require that we depend on training principles as well as specific responses to specific cues.

Staying safe

One of the first rules of safety is: **Ride where you can, not where you can't**. If you are riding a horse who has a tendency to spook, make sure that you are riding in an environment in which you can control the horse.

If the horse startles and steps sideways, and you can ask him to stop or to do some maneuver like turning or putting his head down, and he'll do it every time within two or three steps, then it may be safe to take the horse on the trail.

But, if he shies, then dances a few steps before running away, he is out of control and you shouldn't be on the trail with him. You should be riding in an arena or enclosed pasture until you are sure you have him under control. It may sound like I'm being hard on this point, but people think because the horse is under control most of the time it's OK to take a risk that the few times he is out of control nothing bad will happen. That's foolishness. We wouldn't drive at freeway speed knowing that one time out of 40 the brakes may fail, and we shouldn't ride in circumstances that could get us hurt — even if there's only a one-in-40 chance.

SCARY OBJECTS ON THE TRAIL ARE LIKE LITTLE POP QUIZZES. THEY GIVE US A CHANCE TO SEE IF THE HORSE CAN PAY ATTENTION TO OUR CUES DESPITE DISTRACTIONS.

It's natural

The horse's natural reaction to a scare is to spin around and make a hasty exit. **We can't punish him for doing what comes naturally, but we can train him what to do when he is scared. We can also so condition him to our cues that he gives us the right response automatically — just as he responds automatically to the scare.**

Who spooked first?

If we find ourself noticing every little potentially scary object and tensing in case the horse spies it also, we'll be teaching our horses to spook. **Before long we'll have trained our horse to be a pointer**

It's important to periodically get a horse excited in a controlled environment, so he'll know how to listen to you when he gets excited on the trail. Working at speed is always exciting to a horse.

— pointing out every approaching school bus or garbage can in a new location.

The better we concentrate on our riding, focusing on asking the horse to do what we want him to do — walk this speed, step left, step right and so forth, the more the horse's attention will focus on us. We'll become more important to him than the distractions.

Ride the horse you are on

Now, you say, "John, what other horse would I be riding?" But you'd be surprised how many people aren't realistic about the training level and capabilities of the horse they are on.

Just because you taught your old horse to cross a creek without balking, it doesn't mean that your new one will do the same. So too, just because you could ride along on your old horse with the reins drooping and expect the horse to stay out of trouble, it doesn't mean you can do that with your new horse. And just because a friend's horse can stop on a dime, it doesn't mean your horse is trained well enough to respond to your cue that quickly or consistently. **If we ask the horse to perform above his training level, we are looking for problems.**

What do you want him to do?

If you are not asking the horse to do something, keeping his attention on you, he's likely to find something else to pay attention to — another horse, a nibble of grass, a jack rabbit or something else that you'd rather he not react to. Give him a job, and he'll have less free time to get into trouble.

He can't be involved in working on giving to the bit or canter departs and still be paying attention to stuff going on around him. He may at first, but as you continue to work on performance, his attention will shift to you.

When a horse shies at something, like a mailbox, what does conventional wisdom tell the rider to do? Go put the horse's nose on the mailbox — show him there's nothing scary about the mailbox. That would be fine if your objective was to have the horse put his nose on every mailbox you came to, but if your objective is to get the horse to walk past mailboxes, then work on your objective.

Practice getting the horse to walk calmly by the mailbox, but 50 feet away from it. Continue working with the horse, asking him to do something you want him to do, like soften his neck, or walk slower or faster, and work your way past the mailbox, 40 feet away, then 30 feet, then 20 feet and so forth until you reach your goal — walking right next to the mailbox without his flinching. Then you'll have done two things — improved the response you were working on (the "give" or speed control) and taught your horse to focus on you, not the distraction.

Pop quiz time

Would it be easier to take a big exam from a teacher who gave lots of pop quizzes, so you knew what type of questions would be asked, or from someone who never gave a test all semester but graded the whole course on one exam? Of course, the one who gave pop quizzes. **You'd think of the quizzes as opportunities to prove to yourself that you knew the material and as confidence builders telling you how you'd fare on the big test.**

If the rider's attention wanders, he'll become inconsistent in his cues — making requests and releasing at random times. The horse's performance, naturally, will become inconsistent, also.

Well, scary objects on the trail are like little pop quizzes. They give us a chance to see if the horse can pay attention to our cues despite distractions. Assuming that we are riding in an area where we have control, we can expose our horse to little distractions, such as a horse going the other direction or a person on a bicycle, to see how he will react. No sense waiting until the big trail ride to find out that he's afraid of something — so afraid that he fails the test.

Quick fixes lead to trouble

No one would argue if I suggested that a suitable goal was to have a calm, well-trained horse. Yet lots of times we feel pressed to meet a short-term goal at the expense of what we know to be valuable. We make a big crisis out of something like crossing a creek, now, today, on this trail ride — at the expense of our horse's overall performance.

We may have spent hours teaching him the "speed up" cue, but in one ride we can also teach him our legs don't mean anything, when we kick him and stop kicking him indiscriminately. We may have done thousands of baby gives, asking the horse to give to the bit and releasing when he does, only to blow our cue by dragging our horse up a hill by the reins instead of just leading him, because we are in a hurry.

You must realize that your horse and the overall goal for him is more important than the short-term pressure to perform at any given moment. **That may mean letting the rest of the trail ride go on without you while you practice what your horse is having difficulty with.** Make the ride fun for both of you. Don't let the pressure you feel put him under pressure he's not ready to deal with. You are only asking for a wreck.

Calm down now

When a movie director wants to stop the filming, he yells, "Cut!" and everything shuts down. Do you have a signal you can give your horse and have him calm down? If not, you are potentially out of control at any moment. No matter how much you think your horse appreciates your petting his neck, or reassuring him that everything's OK, that will not work in every situation. **When his head is up, neck tensed, about to make his big exit, you need a no-nonsense cue that will run interference with his hormones telling him to run for his life.** Teach him the "calm down" cue.

IF YOU ARE RIDING A HORSE WHO HAS A TENDENCY TO SPOOK, MAKE SURE THAT YOU ARE RIDING IN AN ENVIRONMENT IN WHICH YOU CAN CONTROL THE HORSE.

The "don't shy" cue

There is no such thing as a "don't shy" cue. In fact, we really can't tell our horse "Don't" and expect performance. We can only tell him what we want him to do. We can't say "Don't run off," but we can say,"Walk this way" or "Turn left, then trot." We replace the behavior we don't want with behavior we want.

But we can only do that once we've trained him to know what walk, trot or turn left cues are. We can only do that when we have trained ourselves to be consistent, thinking riders. If we follow these training principles we'll find we don't need a "don't shy" cue, because we won't be dealing with shying problems.

Dealing with shying

I'm pretty frustrated. Every time I ride my horse on the trail, he spooks. When my trainer rides him, he doesn't spook. She says he's perfect for her, and I must make him nervous. SL/BelAir, MD

In all probability, the horse spooks with your trainer also; she just doesn't recognize it. She picks up on the spook or shy so early that it doesn't look like it even happened.

We've been told that "If I'm calm, my horse will be calm" — but that theory really doesn't hold water. Just because I'm calm, Susie, my wife, isn't necessarily calm. When I'm driving, Susie may get upset and say, "Slow down, we're going too fast." If I tell her to be calm because I am calm, she's NOT going to get calm. She'll probably say, "Of course, you're calm. You're an idiot, and you don't know we're going to die." Just like any normal wife, Susie has spent the last 28 years trying to convince me that just because I feel one way doesn't mean that she has to feel that way. So my calmness does not get her calm, anymore than your trainer's calmness is the only reason your horse doesn't seem to be afraid.

Now, I can alleviate Susie's fears by telling her, "It's OK, I've been through this and everything is going to be fine." I can help her if she's on the borderline. Or I can make it worse. If she's apprehensive — and I say, "Gee, Susie I don't know what's going to happen. Maybe we are going to wreck." — we'll end up playing off each other and both end up scared.

This same thing can happen when riding. A confident rider can help a horse calm his nerves — so that if a school bus goes by, it looks like nothing happened — and the horse doesn't get scared. The experienced rider recognizes the approaching bus as potentially scary, so without even thinking about it, he picks up on the rein, moves the horse over, speeds him up or slows him down a little bit, moves him to the right a step or two, or otherwise directs the horse. The bus goes by. The horse is focused on the rider's request, and the rider doesn't think his horse spooks at school buses.

But, if the rider is a little tense anyway, then the horse starts to ask the rider, "What's wrong?" The rider gets more tense and doesn't concentrate on asking the horse to do what he wants the horse to do, but focuses instead on the approaching bus. The horse says, "This big yellow thing must be something to be afraid of." And the horse visibly spooks.

The more we can focus our horse's attention on what we want him to do, the less we'll have to worry about what he may do on his own. It might be that you are contributing to your horse's nervousness, but this is something you can overcome. Concentrate on a series of exercises, like giving to the bit or asking the horse to drop his head (the "calm down" cue), so that when you first sense something that worries you and might worry your horse, you can make sure the horse is under your control, doing what you want. PH

10

A Horse's Attention:
The Last Thing You'll Get

*First comes the rider's concentration,
then the rider's consistency, then the horse's
performance and, finally, the horse's attention.*

I used to think that the most sophisticated form of riding was bridleless, that not even using reins would be the kindest form of communication with the horse. But I've changed my thinking. After 18 years of riding Zip bridleless, I've discovered that the reins, properly used, are really the most gentle and sophisticated form of communicating with the horse. I still occasionally ride Zip bridleless in demonstrations, but when I went back to using the bridle, I had to retrain him to give to the bit. Understanding the giving concept and your responsibility in it will revolutionize your horse's performance.

"Giving to the bit" is probably one of the most misunderstood terms in the horse industry. To some it refers to the horse's head position or head set; to some it has something to do with steering; but to most it is a vague term that implies the horse obeys signals from the reins. My clinic participants are amazed that they spend three full days learning about giving to the bit — and by the end of the course they realize they have just scratched the surface. Even after working with it for so many years, what I know about the topic is like a thimble or a little plastic film canister relative to a big water trough. It's a big topic.

Before we even talk about the horse, we have to talk about the rider. The rider's concentration always precedes the horse's performance. The clinic participants don't just spend three days learning about giving to the bit; they spend three full days getting the hang

The adage says that first you have to get their attention. John says that you get the horse's performance before you get his attention.

of concentrating on what they are asking the horse. The first thing we have to do is concentrate on one thing. When you don't concentrate, you send inadvertent signals to your horse. Those signals are killers of performance. Your concentration builds your consistency. **When your signals get consistent long enough, your horse will start to get consistent in his performance. Finally, you'll have the horse's attention.** His attention always comes after his performance.

Giving to the bit is basically the horse recognizing a request the rider makes through the reins and responding to that request by turning control over a part of his body to the rider. It is a psychological thing as well as a physical response. A horse with a perfect headset may not be giving to the bit at all. Giving to the bit implies responsibility on the part of both the rider and the horse. Let's look at how it works.

Recognition, response and control

Giving to the bit is made up of three components: recognition, response and control — in that order. If you saw a twenty-dollar bill on the sidewalk, you would stop and pick it up because you recognized it as valuable. If a little child saw both a shiny quarter and an old twenty-dollar bill, they'd pick up the quarter. They would not recognize the bill as important. We want our horses to recognize us as important.

Once you recognized the money as important, you'd move to pick it up; that's the response. You'd have turned over control of a part of your body — your hand — to that $20. That bill got you to stop your feet, then lower your head, and for one instant it had enough control that you reached down to grasp it and put it in your pocket. When the money controlled your hand, it also stopped your feet.

Let's convert the analogy into dealing with the horse. Assume we are the money on the ground, waiting for the horse to recognize us. Waiting for the horse's response is unnatural, but we have to do it if we want a willing partner. No one twisted your arm to get you to pick up the money; you recognized it as valuable and responded accordingly. If we force our horse's response, we will always have to force the response. **We have to change our mind set from that of making the horse do something, or enforcing a behavior, to setting up a request that the horse sees as worth responding to.**

How this happens

First, in order to ask the horse to respond, or "give," you have to have a motivator, a reason for the horse to change what he is doing. (**A motivator doesn't necessarily cause the change that you want; it just inspires change or movement.** The change can be anything from the horse lowering his head to picking up his right foot, or stiffening his back, or moving his hindquarters.) The motivator that we will use is the threat, or the carrying out of the threat, of taking all the slack out of the reins.

Remember, when we taught the horse to accept the bridle, we motivated him to open his mouth by our putting one finger in his mouth. We didn't hurt him; we just slipped our finger inside and waited. It didn't take long because the horse's first thought was to spit out our finger. The horse made a change in the position of his mouth and the action of his jaw and tongue. Our finger in his mouth inspired the horse to make a change, just as picking up on the rein will.

When you have contact with the horse's mouth or the threat of contact with the horse's mouth, what you are doing is, in effect, putting your fingers in the horse's mouth. For all he cares, the reins and bit don't exist; just you being in his mouth matters. The horse doesn't like it. If I did that to you, your thoughts wouldn't be on the phone bill or the dinner you are planning to make; you'd think, "How can I get his hand out of my mouth?" That's what will motivate, or inspire, the horse to do something different.

So, we've created change. How do we tell the horse when he's made the change that we want? We use the "yes" cue. **When the horse does something and we release the rein, it's like we're telling him, "Yes, that's it!"**

The "yes" cue becomes a reason for the horse to repeat the change he made. Let's talk about the horse moving his head. He can move his head up, down, left, right and combinations of those directions. How does he know which way you want him to move? We tell him with the "yes" cue. We've already discussed that the horse doesn't want our hand in his mouth, so taking our hand out of his mouth, as it were, is something he wants.

GIVING TO THE BIT IS BASICALLY THE
HORSE RECOGNIZING A REQUEST THE
RIDER MAKES THROUGH THE REINS AND
THEN RESPONDING TO THAT REQUEST BY
TURNING CONTROL OVER A PART OF HIS
BODY TO THE RIDER.

Say your horse is tossing his head around, and he is already on a loose rein; he has no incentive to change what he is doing. As he starts to throw his head up and down, you threaten to, or actually do, take all the slack out of the rein, trying to inspire a change in his behavior. As soon as his head is quiet for one-tenth of a second, you release the rein (the "yes" cue). He has gotten a reward for keeping his head quiet for that tenth of a second.

The release of the rein is the reason you get consistency in your horse's performance. The release is the pay check. If you don't provide the pay check, there's no reason for him to show up to work. **Even after you have him trained, if you quit releasing the rein when he does what you've asked, it's guaranteed he's going to stop doing whatever you were asking him to do.**

And, just as you might move quicker to pick up a fifty-dollar bill than a one-dollar bill, the quicker you give your horse the release of the rein — the pay check — the quicker he'll respond in the future.

Through the motivator and the "yes" cue, you can talk to every part of the horse, just as the $20 spoke to your eyes, feet, hands and so forth. The "right answer" cue has to come immediately after the action. You owe it to your horse to give him a clear answer.

Why not use a stronger bit?

There are folks who say, "You bet I want my horse to recognize me as important. He'd better, or else." "Or else" won't train a horse. You can't get consistently good performance from a horse on the basis of pain. That's why it's counterproductive to use strong bits. You can't create a relaxed performance by giving a horse pain. The horse learns to be confident in responding to your request by the release, just as you learn to be confident in your job when you get paid.

A general request will get a general response. A specific request will get a specific response. As we learn to teach the horse to give to the bit, we'll be getting very specific. In fact, we'll be looking at getting specific muscles to respond, not just getting the horse to cooperate with us.

If you were trying to decipher a message in a foreign language, and you didn't know the language, there are a few things you could figure out. If the lines were faint and wiggly, you might think the person was weak and frail, or you might think that the lead in his pencil was wobbly. If the message was written in very bold ink with capital letters, it might seem like the writer was yelling at you.

When the horse tries to crack the code, he can guess some information, but he needs the specifics; he needs to learn that "h—a—y" means hay, dinner. If today it means hay and tomorrow it means go to the gate, you'll have a very confused horse. If he stands there trying to figure it out, he runs the risk of being called stubborn. If he heads toward the barn, so he doesn't get in trouble for just standing there, he gets punished for not going to the gate. It can get extremely complicated if we are not specific in our message.

Try this exercise at home. Have someone stand in front of you. Tell them this exercise has to do with their right foot, but don't tell them anything else. Tap their shoulder lightly (the motivator) with a riding crop or whip until they move their foot to the right (the response you want). Most likely, they'll move it up and down, forward, back, roll over on the side of their foot, etc. before stepping to the right.

The moment they step to the right, stop tapping. Repeat the exercise.

Now imagine the horse. You can't tell him that this has to do with his right foot. You use the motivator, taking the slack out of the rein, then you just wait for him to respond and turn over control of one part of his body. But which part? You are just asking him to move something. He may move his ears, or his feet, or his tail, or relax his neck, or pull in his belly and move his jaw, or all of those things at once as you release the rein to tell him that he got the right answer. But which of those was what you had in mind? **Repeat the request, making sure to release the moment the horse guesses correctly. It takes lots of times to isolate which response you are paying him for.**

The average rider thinks that if he's asked the horse to do something several times, and he's responded correctly, that the horse knows what the rider wants. Then the situation changes, or they ride to a different end of the arena. The horse gives the response that he gave earlier, and the rider doesn't pay up. The rider thinks the horse is being stubborn. In reality, the horse tried, but because the signals weren't clear enough or the sequence repeated enough for the horse to isolate the response, he didn't give the answer that the rider wanted.

Developing concentration is probably the most difficult thing for a rider to do. Here John asks Seattle to "give to the bit" in a more advanced maneuver — elevating his forehand. If John is inconsistent, Seattle will become confused and frustrated.

The "release" is the most important part of communicating any request. If the rider doesn't release to tell the horse he did what the rider asked, the horse won't know to repeat the action next time he's asked to do so.

Horses have try, just like we do, and they have give up, just like we do. If we don't make our signals clear, we discourage the horse, and he'll quit trying. On the other hand, if we are generous and tell him when he's on the right track, he'll be encouraged to keep on trying to work it out. You are asking him to crack a code. The closer you give him a "yes" to when he did it right, the quicker he's going to learn the code. ▣

Notes

11

Sweetie Pie And J. Seezher

or ... what to do if your horse kicks
or bites other horses on the trail.

an you: Chew gum? Chew gum and walk? Chew gum, walk and talk to a friend? Chew gum, walk, talk to a friend and pat your head? Chew gum, walk, talk to a friend, pat your head and rub your stomach? Chew gum, walk, talk to a friend, pat your head, rub your stomach and play hopscotch? Pretty soon, you'll say, "John, I can't do all those things — I'll have to give up chewing gum."

If I wanted you to stop chewing gum, the most effective way would not be to yell, "Don't chew gum." That would mean my attention was on the gum, and I'd also be drawing your attention to the gum. **I'd be making a big deal about the thing I want you to forget about doing.** Instead, I'm going to ignore the gum and have you replace chewing it with a more desirable behavior, like playing hopscotch.

How many families have gone through this with nail biting? A child is preoccupied with biting his nails, and pretty soon, telling him to stop biting his nails is a family hobby — to no avail. But, now nail biting is taking up the attention of the entire family. **Saying "don't" doesn't change behavior.** Giving the child's hands another job, however, means they won't be in his mouth. The child isn't biting his nails while he's busy playing the piano or absorbed in a video game.

When your horse is doing something bad, like kicking another horse while you are on the trail, he's telling you he has enough time and energy to both go down the trail and kick another horse, just

These horses are enjoying roughhousing in the field. This ears-back behavior is suitable here, but not suitable once under saddle. When being ridden, the horse should have 100 percent of his attention on the rider and not on the horses around him.

like when you had time to talk with a friend, walk and chew gum. When that happens, you, the rider, have an excuse to ask for something more from your horse.

The key to dealing with the horse who is behaving badly, like laying ears back at another horse passing by, is for the rider to think ahead of the horse, and to replace behavior that isn't wanted with behavior that is. Let's look at a scenario that is actually fairly common.

The story

Your horse, Sweetie Pie, is the most obliging horse anyone knows. She just loves people and seems willing to do whatever you want her to do. But out in the pasture, she is the one who always gets pushed around and beaten up. She has never even imagined what it would be like to have her hay all to herself.

One day, you take Sweetie to another farm to ride in the arena. She is pretty scared. She doesn't necessarily jump around much or get too spooky, but her heart sure beats fast. You are riding around, and one of your friends is riding around on his horse, J. Seezher.

You and Sweetie have never seen JS before, and he isn't paying much attention to you either, as he's absorbed in listening to his rider.

Now, J. Seezher is top in his herd. He hasn't kicked anyone in years, because he hasn't had to — the other horses automatically clear out of his way. JS's rider is working hard, teaching JS to give to the bit. They are into it.

You and Sweetie are just riding along, and JS and his rider are working in a big circle. **JS comes toward Sweetie, and Sweetie's heart beats faster as she steps a bit to the side.** JS continues his circle, now turning away from Sweetie. Sweetie breathes a sigh of relief. You never even noticed, because you are busy trying to get your stirrup to hang straight.

THE LOW-RANKING HORSE, LIKE A CHARACTER FROM THE OLD WEST WHO POINTS THE RIFLE OUT THE WINDOW BEFORE HE EVEN KNOWS WHAT A STRANGER WANTS, KEEPS UNFAMILIAR HORSES AWAY FROM HIS BUDDY AND IS MOST AGGRESSIVELY DEFENSIVE.

JS comes back again toward Sweetie as he does his circle. Sweetie's heart beats fast again, but this time she doesn't move away. JS moves away at the direction of his rider, who never even noticed you and Sweetie. Sweetie is a bit confused, but glad she "dodged the bullet." And the pattern repeats itself two or three more times.

By the fourth time, Sweetie has it in her mind that maybe JS is moving away from her because he sees her as top dog. After all (this is a mind-blowing concept to her, but it might just be her lucky day), no one knows her here — maybe JS thinks *she* is the top horse. He doesn't know that her herd assigned her the bottom spot. Maybe...

Sure enough, he turned away again. The fifth circle, Sweetie is standing a little taller than previously, and, as she sees JS approach, she makes a plan. Just as he nears her, she throws one ear back, then forward, quickly. Sure enough, JS turns away. Yes — that's it!

This rider knows she has a horse who is easily distracted, so she concentrates on keeping his attention focused on her and giving him lots of little jobs to do.

Now, of course, JS, who is 100 percent involved in paying attention to his rider (and probably wouldn't be distracted by someone like Sweetie, anyway), is unsuspectingly reinforcing Sweetie's delusion.

The sixth circle, Sweetie is ready — this time both her ears go back as JS approaches. JS leaves. Sweetie thinks this is great. The seventh time, she gives an ugly look and ears back. Same result. The eighth time around, **Sweetie lunges at JS, her mouth open, barely missing the rider's leg**, and causing J. Seezher to make his only retreat as an adult horse.

You, the clueless rider (excuse the implication, but if you didn't catch Sweetie before now, you might call yourself clueless) are aghast! You scold Sweetie and apologize profusely to your friend, protesting that Sweetie never did anything like that before.

You are probably right; Sweetie may not have ever acted out like that before, but if you haven't been training her to concentrate on you all the time, she has been thinking about the other horses nearly all the time you've ever ridden her.

Now, if you identify with Sweetie's rider in this story, take heart. Just as we can't train the nail-biting child by saying "Don't," we can't train the horse by saying "Don't." And telling yourself "Don't" won't help, either. Here's what you'll do.

Back to real life

Think ahead of your horse. **Before you even get on the horse, have a lesson plan in mind.** This is true if you are going on the trail or riding in the ring. Have in mind a series of little movements you can ask your horse to do. If you don't already have your horse responding to cues and getting little movements from him regularly, then your lesson plan becomes, "Today, I'm going to work on getting him to move to the left," or "Today, we are going to work on going from trot to walk."

Watch your horse's ears to get an idea of his attention span. **If you lose his attention in five seconds, ask him to do something every three seconds.** It can be anything that gets his response — walk a little faster, move your hip to the right, give to the left rein, walk slower, turn around a bush and so forth.

When your horse's ears tell you that he is distracted by another horse or by an object in his vicinity, immediately ask him to do something for you. It will take discipline on your part to keep your attention on what you are asking your horse to do, instead of on the distraction.

The same thing applies to the horse who wants to go out the gate. You can spend a lifetime telling him, "Don't look out the gate; don't even think about it," but then both of you would be focused on the gate. Instead, give yourselves another focus, say, changing the speed of the trot, six steps medium trot then six steps slow trot. You will have accomplished three things. You will have been working on speeding up and slowing down, you will be getting your horse used to being responsive to you, and neither of you will be thinking about the gate.

Giving ugly looks

Now, back to the horse giving ugly looks. This is a serious thing. **Horses who give ugly looks aren't making idle threats.** They are truly saying, "I'm going to kick your head off," or "I'm going to eat you for lunch." **The more often they think those thoughts, the more likely they will act on their thinking.**

The horse who lays his ears back or kicks at another horse on the trail is dangerous. Not only will he injure another horse or himself at some point, but he's likely to injure a rider — either with a direct blow, or the other horse, in evading your horse, may end up injuring his rider.

Horses don't bluff. **If your horse lays his ears back at another horse, take immediate action, not to punish him, but to replace his unwanted behavior with a wanted behavior.** If you give him enough good things to do, he won't have time to carry out the bad, and eventually he'll quit thinking about them.

And, by the way, it's rarely the top horse in the herd who gets aggressive in a riding situation. It's the lowest in the pecking order who is always on the defensive and thus becomes aggressive, making a move to chase other horses away before they push her around. The low-ranking horse, like a character from the old West who points the rifle out the window before he even knows what a stranger wants, keeps unfamiliar horses away from his buddy and is most aggressively defensive. That's the horse you most need to teach to focus on you, 100 percent of the time. PH

12

Why A Snaffle Bit?

There's no magic in any bit. Bits are simply tools we use to communicate with our horses, just as we use the phone to talk with our friends.
So why do we recommend a full cheek snaffle?

W alk into any tack store and just look at the variety of bits — all to put into the mouth of one kind of animal. Each type represents a particular idea of how to control a horse. You can buy curb bits, Walking Horse bits, gag bits, hackamores, mechanical hackamores, kimberwickes, pelhams, grazing bits ... the list is nearly endless. Even within each type, some represent fabulous craftsmanship and some are crudely made, some fancy and some utilitarian.

I bypass everything but a broken-mouth, full cheek snaffle, because to me it represents the tool that can communicate the best with the least amount of discomfort to the horse.

Before I detail why I think the snaffle bit is the best tool, let's look at why we use bits at all, and some common misconceptions about bitting.

Bits don't train horses. People train horses. The only reason we use a bit is as a communication device, and with it we can develop a language that makes sense to both us and the horse. If we want a horse to change what he's doing, he needs not only a signal that we want him to change something, but a reason to make a change, a motivator. Now, while pain can motivate a horse, it is not the best motivator. Whenever you deal with a horse, pain or discomfort is a distraction; so, aside from the humane reasons to minimize the discomfort you cause a horse, any level of pain interferes with performance. **The more pain and the more unpredictable the pain,**

When choosing a full cheek snaffle bit, be sure that the metal is smooth and there are no rough edges to irritate the horse's mouth.

the more excited or fearful the horse becomes and the harder he is to control.

So, what we want to do is find something that the horse cares about to motivate him. For example, when a child has a favorite TV program, the parents may use that show as a reward — "If you get your room cleaned up, you can watch the show."

What the horse cares most about is his mouth being free. If we put our hand in the horse's mouth — i.e., apply pressure on the reins — the thing he wants most is our hand out of his mouth. So we use that as a reward — "If you slow your feet, then I'll take my hand out of your mouth."

Developing responsiveness

Obviously, since our goal is to get performance, from either the child or the horse, we'll want to use only the motivational pressure that gets that job done, and no more. When the child knows that the parent is going to hold the line and be faithful to the agreement about the room and TV, and that there's no compromise on that point, then she gets to where she's asking mom to come check out her room, and reminding mom that the show is coming on soon.

That's what happens with the horse, also. The rider teaches the horse the "giving to the bit" exercises, and the horse learns that no matter what, the rider is going to adhere to the agreement, which includes an immediate and consistent release of the rein when the horse complies with the rider's request. **Pretty soon, the horse begins to respond as the rider reaches for the rein. That's when we talk about the horse being responsive or having a light mouth.** It's what makes riding safe and pleasurable, and it's the foundation for advanced performance.

A bit doesn't mechanically slow a horse down. Horses must be taught what the use of the bit means and must have an incentive to respond to its message. But, novice riders generally don't understand this and think of the reins and bit as brakes, that somehow pulling on a bit mechanically affects a horse's speed. You can see horses being ridden for the first time having their mouths pulled on, as if the reins could stop the horse. Most experienced riders know that a horse can "run through the bridle," that is, ignore the hardest pull of the reins. But, if the horse doesn't slow down in response to the pull, riders often pull harder.

Leveraging strength

The reins and a bit are the extension of the rider's hand. A rider can't reach around and put his hand in the horse's mouth, so he uses an extension. But a bit is more than just that. It can operate like a hydraulic jack and leverage a rider's strength. You can't lift a horse trailer with your bare hands, but with a jack you have more than enough strength. With a leverage bit in the horse's mouth, you multiply your strength so that you can cause more pain than you can with your hands alone. **Of course, the only problem is that when you operate with a system that involves strength and pain, you have to keep increasing the pain to maintain effectiveness — which we are not about to do.**

That is not to say that well-trained, thoughtful responsive riders using leverage bits always cause their horse pain, but the system isn't optimal. The more potential for causing pain to the horse, the more responsibility the rider has to use that tool carefully. Given that the most difficult task I've done in working with thousands of horses and riders is training the rider to be consistent, it was important to me to develop a system that would prevent the horse pain, prevent rider frustration, and would keep them both safe. So, I turned to the full cheek snaffle.

Changing direction

It is easier for a horse in motion to change direction than it is to halt. With the snaffle bit, we can change the horse's direction when we cannot get his feet to stop. Instead of depending on a device that causes the horse pain and attempts to somehow crunch him into compliance, the snaffle bit allows the rider to steer the horse.

When a horse changes directions, he also has to slow his feet for a split second. We can build on that because the horse will begin to pause before changing directions. In time, he'll stop his feet the moment you reach for the rein.

Relaxing the neck

Beyond just changing direction with the snaffle, we can use it to ask the horse to soften his neck muscles. When a horse stiffens a muscle, he locks us out of access to that muscle. His body stiffens, and performance suffers. He'll be just a little slower around a turn, or stiffer coming off the ground if he's jumping, or slower making transitions, or harder to stop.

All bits and hackamores put pressure somewhere on the horse's head or in a combination of places on his head, when the rider pulls on the reins.

ILLUSTRATION BY SUSAN HARRIS, TAKEN FROM THE CHA COMPOSITE HORSEMANSHIP MANUAL, COURTESY OF CHA. 800-399-0138

Any bit, such as a straight bit, curb bit or a snaffle, allows the horse to lean against it when both reins are held taut. **All horses have a tendency to get heavy on the bit.** When the horse gets heavy on the bit, he uses it (and us) to balance himself, and by taking the slack out of the rein himself and tensing his neck, he removes the possibility of our jerking on his mouth.

Let's look for a moment at how a horse balances against the bit. When a horse runs, body tension puts his whole skeleton in a straight line so he can

A horse uses his head and neck to help his balance, especially in motion. When the rider pulls on the reins, even the most obedient horse will stiffen his neck and pull against the rider.

push away from the ground with maximum force. He stiffens his neck, using it for balance, and pushes down and forward with his head, like you would do if hiking a steep trail with a pack on your back.

So, any bit that works from front to back on a horse, like a curb bit, will eventually allow the horse's neck to stiffen, and, sooner or later, the horse will get heavy on the bit.

Only one rein

We always speak about picking up the rein, not the reins, because when we use only one rein and release it at the end of each request, the horse becomes responsible for his own balance, which means, in addition to improved performance, he'll be more sure-footed and the rider will have better balance, as well.

If you pull back on both reins, you give the horse something to lean against, a way to increase his speed. You'll have a stiff-necked, unresponsive horse. That's why, when using a snaffle bit, the more out-of-control a horse is, the more imperative it is that you use one rein to control him.

How a full cheek snaffle works

We've determined that a bit is a motivator and that the snaffle allows us to change the horse's direction or ask him to soften his neck muscles, preventing him from bracing against the bit. So, why a full-cheek snaffle?

When the rider picks up on the right rein, the cheek pieces on the left side will encourage the horse to turn his nose to the right.

We know that, when you pull on the rein, a snaffle bit works by putting pressure on the horse's lips. But, the full cheek snaffle goes a step beyond. **When you pull on the left rein of a snaffle bit, the right cheekpiece presses against the right side of the horse's face.** Most people think that they are pulling the left jaw to the left. In actuality, they are pushing the right jaw toward the left, in effect herding the jaw in the direction they want it to go.

Try this yourself. Place your right index finger along the right side of your jawbone. Use your finger to push your jaw to the left. That's how the right side of a full cheek snaffle works when you pull on the left rein.

Of course, the natural inclination is for the horse to "push against the push" — that is, to try to nudge the bit away, instead of turning his nose left. But, as he learns to "give to the bit," he learns to move away from that pressure and turn his nose left.

For ease of discussion, we've been talking about pulling on one rein or another. In reality, the rider shouldn't be pulling on a rein, but merely taking the slack out of it. A horse who is repeatedly pulled on learns to pull on the rider. If a rider doesn't take slack out of the rein smoothly, but instead gathers the rein quickly and, in doing so, jerks on the horse's mouth, the horse will lean on the bit, taking the slack out of the rein himself to keep from getting jerked on. It's easier for him to deal with constant pressure than a jerk (a quick movement of the rein).

But, what do we do if our riding discipline or showing style requires the use of a bit other than a snaffle? Beyond training the horse most efficiently, we can look at the "giving to the bit" exercises as a way of loosening up our horse's neck and developing performance. **It allows us to train for performance beyond what we'll ask for in the show ring.**

For instance, one upper-level dressage rider reported that after warming up using the "giving to the bit" exercises, then working on flying lead changes in her usual manner, the horse was lighter and more responsive than he'd ever been before. That was because **he had a chance to loosen up and warm up all those neck muscles and develop a rewarding "conversation"** with his rider prior to the more-demanding work.

Other riders who show in Western Pleasure say their horses are considerably lighter on the forehand and present a much smoother picture, including prettier muscle development, as a result of their training the horse with the "giving to the bit" exercises. They warm up using the snaffle but, of course, switch to a show bit for the class.

Let's return to our original question: "Why a snaffle bit?" All bits and hackamores operate on the principle of getting a horse's attention by putting pressure somewhere on the horse's head, or in a combination of places on his head. If all you want to do is signal "red light" to your horse, any bit will do.

But, the snaffle allows us to communicate with our horse's mouth — and through his mouth to his muscles and brain — by relaxation rather than force. **The snaffle allows the horse's jaw to soften, and he can therefore soften and relax elsewhere in his body and become more responsive to our requests.** A leverage bit may get the horse to slow down or even stop, but it does so through force rather than softness, and force causes the horse to stiffen. A horse that is stiff in his body also becomes stiff between his ears, and he tunes out the rider. ■

Notes

13

A Rear-Ending Lesson

*Dramatic to watch, but scary to ride,
rearing is a dangerous behavior. But how can you
teach your horse not to rear,
especially if you are afraid to ride him?*

L ight on his front end. Dances with his front feet. Quick off the ground. Upwardly mobile. Nice words don't make rearing any less scary, hazardous or unwanted. When a horse rears, neither the rider nor the horse is in control. The horse is scared, angry or both, and he's making a move that can put him off balance and the rider in danger. So, riders who get scared when their horse rears — or who are afraid he might rear — have good reason to fear. Rearing is dangerous.

The solution is not for the rider to become more brave or to punish the horse. The horse doesn't want to rear. He's telling the rider, "I don't see any other option."

So, how do you change your horse's behavior, especially if you are not confident in the saddle? As always, when we analyze a problem, we return to basic training principles for guidance.

When a horse does something we don't want him to do, the first thing we should ask ourselves is, what do we wish he was doing instead? It almost sounds too basic, but for anything we want our horse to do, we need a cue or signal. After all, the horse can't read our mind. When a horse rears, his head, neck and front feet go up. We want to be able to tell them to go down. **We want the feet to stay on the ground and the head at a reasonable, controllable height. That becomes our goal.**

However, a goal is not a starting place, so first we must determine where to begin teaching our horse, "Put your head down."

Where to start?

The principle is, "What can we ask the horse to do and have him do it 100 percent of the time?" That's our starting point.

Remember when we were teenagers and wanted our mom to say "yes" to something she was leaning toward saying "no" about? We'd remind her of past circumstances when she had said "yes" and everything had worked out well. We'd then build our case, reminding her of all the times we came home on time, that we didn't wreck the car, that we did the chores she requested before we left, and so forth. By taking her back to a previous time when she said "yes," we would encourage her to say "yes" again.

That's what we do with our horse when we take him back to a point of 100 percent compliance and control. **We ask him questions he answers "yes" to, until he's in the habit of answering "yes" with confidence.**

If there is something he doesn't want to do, or if you put pressure on his mouth, a horse's normal reaction is to bring his head up — sometimes suddenly. The purpose of this lesson is to replace the instinct to go up with a conditioned response to go down.

So, like the teenager listing all the times we complied with mom's wishes, we will brainstorm all the things our horse does perfectly when we ask. Then we'll use one of those exercises as a starting point in our training.

Ride where you can...

Not where you can't. This principle helps us select a safe location to begin, and it applies to ground work as well as riding.

Since our objective is always control, it would be stupid to take an activity in which we had only marginal control and use that as the basis for more advanced training. Yet that's what folks often do, unknowingly. Instead of backtracking to safe, sure territory, they begin in a barely-in-control setting.

For instance, let's say that your horse rears at the end of the driveway. Riding him up to the end of the driveway and then trying to deal with the rearing problem won't work. That's akin to picking a fight, rather than solving a problem.

If my horse reared at the end of the driveway, you wouldn't find me at the end of the driveway until I had extraordinary control in other places. Then, when we returned to the "crime scene," the horse wouldn't notice, because he'd be busy responding to me.

So, I'd go back to a place where I had control and an activity where the horse responded 100 percent of the time. That may be the arena, a favorite spot in the pasture or, depending on the horse, maybe right inside his stall. **Since we have to obey the three rules of horse training — the trainer can't get hurt, the horse can't get hurt, and the horse must be calmer at the end of the lesson than at the beginning — location may be important.**

Meet Lightfoot

To explain the lesson, and give you confidence that you can do this with your own horse regardless of his training, let's work with an imaginary horse we'll call "Lightfoot." We can ride him, but he's not particularly well trained. That is, he doesn't know about leads or giving to the bit, but he goes, stops and turns — sort of — when we ask.

Let's also say that Lightfoot has OK ground manners, but not great. We can lead him, but he bangs into us if he's distracted by something to his right, and occasionally he'll refuse to walk up with us, or might push past us. Now, I hate to tell you this, but I would call

Standing to the left of the horse, John is working on the left rein and watching the horse's left ear, so he can release the moment the ear goes down. Ideally, you would not allow the extra part of the rein to be in a position where the horse could step on it until the horse has learned this lesson thoroughly.

You'll want to do this exercise both pulling up on the rein, as if you were in the saddle, and pulling down, as if on the ground.

Lightfoot an unbroken horse — even if he's 10 years old. However, in this lesson we're not going to deal with all the training he really needs. We're just going to concentrate on creating a safety valve — a cue we can use to demand that his head go down.

Because we're scared of what Lightfoot might do when we're riding him, and because we don't have a round pen or small enclosure in which to work, we're going to begin on the ground, in an arena or pasture. We'll get Lightfoot outfitted with a snaffle bridle (ideally a full cheek snaffle, but that's not critical).

The plan

Any time we want a change from our horse, we ask four questions:
1. What part of the horse do I want to change?
2. In what direction do I want it to change?
3. What is the motivator?
4. What is the "yes" cue? (How will I tell him know that he did what I wanted to do?)

As we stand there to the left of Lightfoot, facing his left shoulder, let's say that the distance between the tip of his left ear and the ground is about six feet. In this case, it's the left ear we want to change, and we want it to go down. (We chose the ear because it's easy to see from the saddle as well as from the ground. Since you're standing on the ground, you could assume we're talking to the nose, since it's the nose we eventually want on the ground.)

The motivator is that we are going to take all the slack out of the rein, essentially like putting our finger in the horse's mouth. He'll want us to release the rein (take our finger out of his mouth), so the tension in the rein is the motivator. The "yes" cue is the release of the rein. **Because what's important to the horse is the release of the rein, our hand position isn't critical**. Now we have a plan.

By the way, this exercise may take as little as 10 minutes or may take much longer, depending on how well you know the lesson, how quickly the horse stumbles onto the right answer, how quickly you release when he gets the right answer, and the individuals involved. Repetition is the key. Regardless of how quickly he seems to understand the lesson, if you can't put him under pressure, as you'll see at the end of this article, then he hasn't learned it.

Putting the plan into action

So, with the horse standing beside us, we'll take all the slack out of the rein, putting just a little downward pressure on it, and hold that pressure steady until we see the horse's ear go down.

The horse will probably turn his head toward us, essentially giving to the bit. But, because that's not what we're asking of him, we're going to continue to hold tension on the rein. He may begin to walk or nudge into us. We're not concerned about where his feet go (keeping ours out from under his, of course). We're waiting for his ear to drop.

It's possible that the horse's ear will not move, and that he'll keep his head at the same elevation, whether his feet move or not. If you think that the horse is actively exploring what you want from him, don't increase the pressure. But if it appears he's just standing there, wait two seconds — count two seconds out loud (one 1,000, two 1,000). If there's no movement within two seconds, increase the pressure on the rein about a pound. Count again. If again no movement, increase pressure on the rein. Keep increasing pressure at two-second intervals until you get movement from Lightfoot's ear.

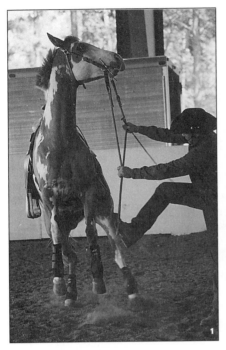

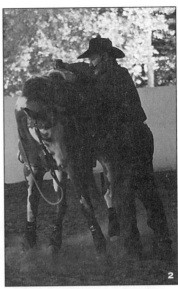

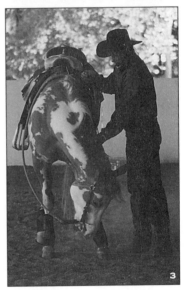

❶ *Just to demonstrate what the horse would do if he stepped on his own rein, John begins to step on the rein. The horse has a pretty dramatic reaction — the same as he'd have on the trail if someone pulled hard on a rein for any reason — like when he wanted to head for home and the rider wanted to stay out on the ride.*

❷ *This exercise may take a fair amount of strength from time to time, as the horse struggles to understand what you want and tries various options.*

❸ *As John stays consistent, releasing when there is a noticeable drop in the height of horse's head — even 1/4", the horse understands what he wants and begins to go through the stages of dropping his head on cue.*

Now, why don't we put a lot of pressure on at first? Because we don't want a big reaction from the horse. We are conducting a lesson, not creating a fight. So **we'll use only the pressure we need to get the response we want.** Later on, once we've thoroughly taught the lesson, we'll occasionally put a lot of pressure on the rein, as a "pop quiz" to see if he knows the lesson and also as a demand cue, a way we can emphatically tell him to drop his head and calm down when he is excited.

We've got movement

Most likely what will happen is that the horse's ear will go up, say, to 7'. We won't release the rein or increase pressure on it. Instead we'll hold tension on the rein until we see a noticeable drop in the ear — at least one-quarter inch. After a moment at 7', or 7'2" , his head will come down to 6' 11 3⁄4". Then we'll release the rein, because his ear will have started down. We'll give him a two-second break, then begin the exercise again. **The longer it takes him to figure out the right answer, the longer time I give him in between requests.** When he's comfortable, ask him again.

When that ear goes down to 6'11 3⁄4", release the rein and congratulate the horse. He'll bring his head back down to 6' on his own as he relaxes. Pick up the rein again. Again his head will go up to 7'. Hold tension on the rein until you feel him thinking about dropping his ear. While later on we will expect the ear to actually drop, initially we want to reward the horse's right thinking. **The quicker we release, telling him he's on the right track, the more confidence he builds and the more quickly we can repeat the question.**

Pretty soon you'll pick up on the rein and Lightfoot's head will only go up to 6' 11 3⁄4", then drop to 6' 11 1⁄2". Congratulations — you're making progress. All this may take some rein shuffling — one hand helping the other — so that you can keep slack out of the rein. Unlike the "giving to the bit" exercise, which does not require you to put much pressure on the bit and where you can brace your hand against the saddle, this exercise requires you to adjust the rein in order to hold tension on it. The horse, in addition to bringing his head up, will probably swing his nose to the side. When that happens, you'll have to continue to take out the slack.

The first 12 inches down may happen in one-quarter or one-half inch increments, but all of a sudden, instead of the horse taking his head up to 6' 11", he'll drop it down to 5' 11", one inch from the 6' starting point. Now he's going down when you pick up the rein.

What went down comes back up

So, obviously you should release the rein when the horse drops his head to 5' 11". And what do you think happens? He relaxes, and brings his head back up to 6'. Our first goal was to get the horse to understand that when we put pressure on the rein, we want his ear to go down. The second is to get the horse to keep his head down.

So, we pick up on the rein, and the horse drops his head to 5' 11", but it comes right back up to 6'. Do you:

A. Hold tension on the rein, or

B. Release the rein?

This is where real thinking comes into play. If we hold, we've changed the language, which will confuse the horse. So, we must release. But at this stage, we must think and work fast.

Once the horse's head was down to the 6" level, John again tried putting pressure on the rein. This time, instead of the head going up to about 7' as it had before (taking the horse's front feet with it), the horse's head only came up to about 3'.

Right, John continues to ask him to drop his head.

We pick up the rein; he goes from 6' to 5' 11 3⁄4"; we release the rein. **The instant he starts back up with his ear, we pick up on the rein, telling him to drop his ear again**. He drops it; we release. The instant he picks it up again, we ask him to drop it again.

He may do this 50 or 100 times. If we let his head stay up for a second or so, he'll have his head back up to the next highest level, and it will take forever (at least it feels that way) to get it lower and lower. So, every time he picks his head up, immediately ask him to drop it again. When he keeps his head at the new lower elevation, allow him to relax with it there. He'll get the idea that that's where you want his head, especially when you ask it go down the moment he tries to bring it back up.

Now, if the horse drops his head in big increments, like in feet instead of inches, then his head will also end up going up in big increments. So, inch-by-inch progress is ideal. Also, we want the horse to respond to the lightest pressure, so all the while see if you can get the same response on lighter and lighter rein pressure.

FYI

Once the horse consistently responds to the rein by dropping his head, and he keeps it down, you can step into the saddle for the rest of the lesson, even allowing the horse to walk, or you can continue the lesson from the ground. If in the saddle, sit tall, so that when you pull on the rein you can keep tension on it without leaning forward.

Between 6' and 5', it's slow going. Suddenly, though, Lightfoot's head will drop to 4'. You'll work at around 4' for a while, and suddenly his ear will drop to 3' — but then you'll hit a plateau. At 3', his head is about level with his forearm, and you'll have to modify your lesson plan. **Instead of just teaching him to drop his head, you'll have to teach him to pull down on the rein.**

("Oh, no, John. I've spent half his and my life trying to get him not to pull on the rein.") It's true, though — you want to teach your horse to pull that rein down. That's because, at about 3', your horse will try to give to the side, again and again. He'll be stuck.

Imagine for a moment that you're calling Lightfoot, and the rein is the phone. When someone calls you, and it seems that no one is on the other end, you say, "Hello? Hello? Is anyone there?" When you don't get an answer, you again say, "Hello? Who's there?" If again you get no answer, you hang up. Well, that's what we want our horse to do, essentially. We'll call him on the rein, and he'll try to give to the side to answer our call — "Hello? Hello, trainer? Lightfoot here. Is anyone there?" We'll hold the same tension on the rein, keeping silent on the other end of the phone. He's looking for a release — for someone on the other end of the phone — but no one's there.

He'll ask again, and again we'll just wait. Finally, he'll get a little frustrated and hang up, which is what we want him to do at this stage of the lesson. **When a horse "hangs up," he'll bring his head forward, and his nose down, taking his ear with it, which is what we want to go down. As soon as it even feels like he's thinking of hanging up, release the rein, letting him take the rein down and out of your hand.** If you don't, he'll begin to hang up, then feel your contact and say, "Oh, you are there."

Now, we don't want the horse to become rude; we just want him to stretch the rein, as it were, out of our hand. If he gets angry and pulls hard, then we'll aim his nose toward his front foot. He can't pull as hard to the side as down.

What if the horse, instead of taking his head down, brings it all the way to the side — like bringing it to your knee if you are riding him? Then, you'll have to push his head forward with the rein. Raise the rein halfway up his neck, and physically push the front part of his neck over with the taut rein. It takes real effort to do this. You'll do the same thing whether you are training on the ground or from the saddle.

Going below three feet

Pretty soon you'll have Lightfoot through the 3' barrier. It will go slowly again, in small increments between 3' and 2', then suddenly you'll get about a 12-inch drop. Then the next six inches may go quickly or take quite awhile, but eventually you'll get to about 6" from the ground and get stuck again. This is where you have to make another modification.

To anyone watching, it will look like you are making fabulous progress, and that just a few more gives down and you'll have it made. But in reality, your horse's head is at 5', even though it looks to be only 6". That's because, when you pick up on the rein and put more pressure on it than you previously have, the horse's head will come up. As it comes up, you should add pressure. The higher his head, the more pressure you will add — not jerky, but smooth

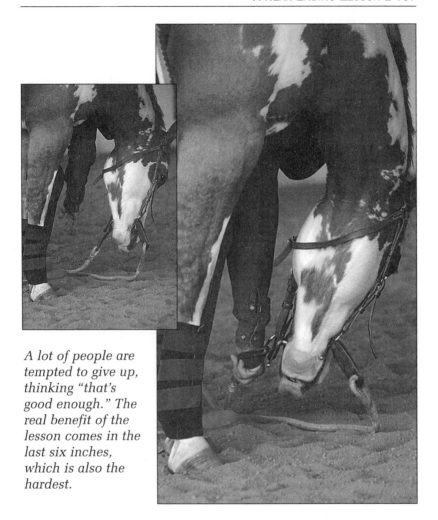

A lot of people are tempted to give up, thinking "that's good enough." The real benefit of the lesson comes in the last six inches, which is also the hardest.

pressure. He'll get his head up to 5', then drop it down again — to 6". Release the rein.

Remember how hard you worked for all the one-quarter-inch drops between 6' and 5'? Then suddenly the horse's head dropped to 4'? Well, Lightfoot is taking you back to fill in the gaps between 5' and 4'.

OK, so you have filled in the gaps all the way down, and now no matter when you pick up the rein, Lightfoot's nose goes to 6" and stays there. If you are riding him, allow him to keep walking even though his nose is only six inches off the ground. Keeping working with the exercise, using the pressure needed to get the response you

Pop quiz: Success is not only going through the entire lesson, but having done it so thoroughly that should someone inexperienced tie a horse by the reins (a pop quiz), a wreck would not result. Instead, the horse would give toward the fence when he felt the pressure on his mouth.

want, actually making the horse a little angry, until he ends up saying, "GIMME THAT REIN!" and takes his head all the way down. You don't want to get him scared or show unwanted behaviors — just annoyed enough to say "OK." Remember that anytime the horse drops his head and leaves it were we want it, we leave him alone, letting him know he's doing the right thing. Incidentally, no matter how well the horse knows how to respond on one rein, going to the other rein will be like starting all over again.

Is the last six inches worth the work?

The last bit sometimes takes the longest, but the real benefits of the lesson are found in the last six inches. When you have worked through the last six inches, when you can pick up the rein and put pressure on it and have your horse drop his nose all the way to the ground — great things also happen:

1. Lightfoot can't rear. He can't take his nose to the ground and bring his front feet very far off the ground at the same time.

2. You'll have a demand cue — something that you can use to demand that Lightfoot drop his head — now. This is what you want when he tries to rear as his buddies leave him behind on the trail, or when he doesn't want to go out the driveway alone. At the horse show when he thinks he'd rather rear than going into the ring, tell him to drop his head. You can also use it when you are leading him and he gets a little "uppity."

3. You have a tool you can use to train Lightfoot's emotions. You can get him excited, like by asking him to move faster, then tell him to drop his head and calm down. As you work his emotional control up and down, you'll be training him to get calm quicker.

4. If Lightfoot decides to jig on the trail, you can use this cue. He can trot with his head down, but he can't jig very well with it down.

5. You'll be strengthening and stretching his back muscles, which is good for all horses — reining, dressage, draft, gaited, you name it. It's a good stretch-and-relax exercise.

6. You'll have also established a safeguard. What would happen if Lightfoot stepped on his reins? Well, if he didn't know how to give down to pressure, his head would jerk up, breaking the reins, scaring him and hurting his mouth. If he has learned this lesson, he'll drop his head to the ground.

Now for a pop quiz

The whole reason we did this lesson was that Lightfoot gets "light on his feet." So, let's see if we have a safety value to prevent that from happening. Assuming that we've taught this lesson from both sides of the horse, that he responds to a pull up on the rein (as if from the saddle) as well as a pull down on the rein (as if he stepped on his own rein), try the pop quiz like you see me doing above. Loop the reins around a secure fence rail (don't tie them!) so when the horse raises his head, he feels a pull on the bit. What is his reaction? If it is to pull back, he has not learned the lesson. If it is to "give" toward the fence, he's got the idea.

You can try similar pop quizzes from the saddle, grabbing the rein and seeing where his head goes. Don't be afraid to grab pretty hard (if he stepped on his rein, it would be a pretty hard pull). Theoretically, according to the way we've taught him, the more intense the pull, the quicker he'll take his head down. That's why we refer to it as a demand cue. When we need to, we can pull hard on the rein (not jerk), and the horse should pull down hard, and calm down.

When you have reversed Lightfoot's natural reaction — when you've replaced his natural tendency to rear or raise his head when he's put under pressure, with a conditioned response to drop his head — you won't ever have to deal with a rearing horse again.

Common questions

■ Do we have to drop his head all the way to the ground every time? No. But after working through the last six inches, and working with various intensities of tension on the rein, when we use the rein, he knows we have the authority (ability) to tell him to calm down, "even if I have to make you put your nose on the ground."

■ How often do I practice this? Rarely. Once the horse will drop his head whenever you ask, use the cue only when you need it.

■ Will the horse have a greater tendency to buck when he can get his head down? No. It really doesn't matter if the horse's head is up or down — he can buck either way. But he's much less likely to buck when he's calm than when he's excited.

■ Does it matter what gait the horse is in when I teach him? No, but the walk is easiest. The faster his feet are going, the harder it is for you to disassociate his feet from his ear going down. Once you've learned the lesson, you can teach a horse in any gait (in a safe area), or from the ground.

You can do the same thing from in the saddle. Here John has Seattle down to the 6" level.

■ Won't the horse get confused between giving to the bit and going down? Initially, maybe. But, just like in school when the student gets confused, the teacher continues to teach until the student understands. You will end up putting more pressure on the rein to demand that the horse drop his head than you would when asking for a give to the side. Also, when you think differently, you are different. And, even though it may seem like the same cue to you, your horse will know the difference.

Rearing-ending overview

■ *Take slack out of one rein (motivator). Horse's head will probably go up (motivator worked). Maintain constant pressure on the rein.*

■ *Pick up rein. Hold rein until horse thinks about dropping his ear. Release. (Becoming more specific.)*

■ *Pick up rein. Hold until visible drop of ear 1/4". Release. Continue pattern.*

■ *Suddenly horse will not raise head when you pick up on rein, but drop it 1/4". Release rein when he drops. Horse's head will come back up to starting point when you release the rein. Pick up the rein, asking for another drop as the horse raises his head. Continue pattern until he keeps it at the lower level.*

■ *When horse gets "stuck" at 3', hold tension on the rein until you think he's thinking of "hanging up the phone," pulling down on the rein instead of "giving," then immediately release.*

■ *When he gets stuck again at 6", put additional pressure on rein. Horse will raise his head. Increase pressure as horse raises his head. When he drops it again, release. Continue this pattern until horse doesn't raise his head as you put pressure on the rein, but instead puts his nose all the way down to the ground.* ■PH■

Notes

14

When Trail Riding Isn't Fun

What do you do if you have "performance problems" on the trail but don't have a trainer, arena or round pen to work in? We'll show you.

TRAINING PRINCIPLES

- Ride where you can, not where you can't.

- What can you ask the horse to do and have him do it 100% of the time? What can you do and be 100% in control?

- Practice being in control, not out of control.

- First get performance, then improve on that performance. We don't care about perfection, we care about improvement.

- Choose one exercise to work on. As you improve a horse's performance in one area, other performance areas automatically improve.

- First comes the rider's concentration, then the rider's performance, then the horse's performance, and finally, the horse's attention.

So, your horse thinks he's a dirt bike when he gets on the trail, refusing to keep a steady speed and bouncing through every turn. Or maybe he thinks he was an antelope in an earlier life and bounds sideways left every time a dog comes out of the bushes. Or maybe he's just a confirmed worrier, biting his nails, as it were, jigging every step and neighing for help. On the other hand, maybe he acts like an old dime-store plug, requiring more and more quarters to keep him going. No matter. You can solve his problem and develop a confident, enjoyable trail horse.

This rider is casually walking her horse toward the hay bales and woods. The horse's attention is focused on what's ahead, so, in the top picture, we see her preparing to ask him to give to the bit.

She approaches the bales again and again, making each time a training opportunity. She asks the horse to give to the bit and to continue walking at a steady speed.

In the bottom picture, she's asked the horse to speed up into a trot as he gives. Now the horse is totally focused on the rider and ignoring the bales (and the dog).

This whole time, the rider has focused on improving the horse's performance, not on the bales. Should a rabbit have run out as they approached, both horse and rider, if they even noticed, would have remained calm and in control.

"Oh, sure," you say, "head back to the round pen. Right?" Not necessarily. The round pen is just a safe place to begin working. If you have a safe place to ride, you may be all set. We can solve many trail riding problems, right in your back pasture.

(Just a note: If your horse is a real spook, you **should** do the spook-in-place work in a round pen, essentially teaching him that it's OK to get scared, but not to move his feet when he gets scared.)

ASKING FOR A "GIVE" IS LIKE RINGING THE PHONE. WE CALL THE HORSE, HE ANSWERS AND ASKS US WHAT WE WANT.

Where, oh where, is his attention?

Let's look at a common situation. Your horse is a Looky-Lou; he gets distracted by every unfamiliar sight. You are never totally out of control, but never feel quite totally in control, either. He trots when you ask him to trot, but his steps are faster than you'd like and, while you've never worried about being able to stop him, downshifting isn't smooth. You say, "If only I could get his attention, we'd have a good ride." Well, the bad news is that the horse's attention is the last thing you ever get. But, the good news is that we have a plan to get it.

First comes the rider's concentration, then the rider's consistency. (Bet you're thinking, "Oh, John. I knew you were going to say that.") **Once you are consistent, then you can work on your horse's performance. When his performance gets consistent, you'll find, all of a sudden, that you have his attention.** So, let's get to work.

One thing at a time

We'll ask ourselves, what we can do with the horse and have him be 100 percent under our control? Also think about the rule: Ride where you can, not where you can't. Those two principles will help us establish a plan of action.

Let's assume that you can ride your horse in the back pasture at a walk and, as long as there are no distractions, he obeys nearly every request. That tells you not to think about working on the trail until his performance in the pasture improves. We'll start out at the walk in a pasture (**no other horses there**) or an arena — somewhere you feel safe.

Giving to the bit

We are going to concentrate on asking the horse to give to the bit. For some reason, when you work on this one exercise, the rest of performance improves. In addition to the horse answering each request with a yes, the exercise itself helps unlocks physical resistance to the rider's signals by relaxing all the muscles in the horse's neck.

Asking for a "give" is like ringing the phone. We call the horse, he answers and asks us what we want, then we're able to tell him because he's waiting for direction. When he does what we want, we hang up the phone, as it were, by releasing the rein. Eventually we can ask our horse to give, or move, any part of his body; asking the horse's jawbone to give, however, is the starting point.

Just to remind you, when we ask for the give, we start with loose reins. Then one hand reaches for one rein. The other hand slides the slack out of that rein as the first hand braces itself against the saddle. Now there is one droopy rein and one rein with contact to the horse's mouth.

Then we wait. The horse may pull his head down or up or to the opposite side. But we still hold and wait. **When the horse moves his jaw energetically to the side where we are holding the rein, we totally release that rein, letting both reins droop momentarily.** Within two seconds, we repeat the process. At this point, as long as you are safe, don't worry about steering. Just concentrate on holding the rein then releasing it when the horse gives to the bit.

Getting excited

We've been working on giving to the bit at the walk out in the middle of the pasture, most probably walking big circles each direction as we work on each rein. We've been working on the horse's performance, and as a result we're starting to get his attention. When we feel our horse striding out pretty well, and giving when we ask at the walk, then we're ready to improve that performance.

You want your trail horse to look around, but you also want him to pay attention to your signals. In these photos, when the horse's head comes up, the rider takes slack out of the rein and waits for him to give. Frequent changes of speed also help develop responsiveness.

In addition to all the control benefits from giving to the bit, look at how beautifully this horse is moving. His body is relaxed and he's able to make big comfortable strides.

We're going to raise the excitement level and work to get the same performance we did when things were calmer. There are two ways to do this. One is to introduce excitement around the horse. The other is to ask him to pick up speed.

Because we do things in lots of little steps, in order to build success on success, we'll start with the lowest amount of excitement and allow our dog, who comes with us on trail rides but never chases the horses, to join us in the pasture.

Now, with the dog along, we'll work on walking and giving. Interestingly enough, we may find that, although our horse knows the dog well, he doesn't give as readily, because he's busy watching the dog. If we were on a trail ride, we might not have noticed that we'd lost the horse's attention, because he wouldn't have done any behavior that we didn't want, like spook. Performance would have suffered without our being aware of it.

So, we realize that we must be more attentive to our horse. Perhaps the times he gets out of control don't happen so suddenly after all. It may be that we have not trained ourselves to recognize the early signs. Back to the rule: First comes the rider's concentration.

Adding speed

When the horse's performance has improved to the level it was before we introduced the dog, we're ready to add a little more excitement — we'll add speed, asking our horse to trot a few steps, then walk.

If you feel you may lose control, or lose that nice relaxed, obedient way of going after 10 strides, then be sure to ask the horse to walk at about five. Remember: **Practice being in control, not being out of control.**

If, on the other hand, his first few trot steps are fast and bumpy, ask him to trot, then walk, then trot again. Repeat this pattern lots of times, and he'll realize it's more work to trot fast, than to trot slower. He'll choose the option with less work.

When he begins to trot faster than you want, who is in control? You guessed it. So, if he wants to trot off at 6 mph, ask him for 7 mph for three strides, then slow back down to 4 mph. As you ask him to change gears, you'll be developing good speed control. By the way, if walk-to-trot is rough, the first few strides in the canter probably aren't much fun, either. When you get the walk-to-trot-to-walk transition smooth as glass, use the same lesson plan for getting the canter comfortable as well.

Throughout all this, you've been asking the horse to "give," as well as make changes of speed. But, only ask the horse to do one thing at a time. For instance, ask him to change direction or to give. As soon as he's done what you've asked, you can ask for the next thing. **As you work through the excitement levels, notice that any time the horse's neck gets stiff and his strides short and bumpy, he's "locked you out," which means you are not in control. Ask him to give to the bit.** You'll find he doesn't "answer the phone" as readily as he did at the beginning of the lesson. Go back to giving exercises until you get good response, then back to your speed-control lesson. It all works together.

Ironically, you'll find that when you ride with one rein at a time, the horse knows he'll get a release of the rein, and you won't find yourself fighting the reins to hold him back. This will take a little practice, but when you get it, you'll be amazed. People report spending years with tight reins on a horse who won't slow down, and within a few sessions of giving to the bit at the walk and trot, they have a different horse under them. And, of course, their horse has a different rider.

When we want to further increase the excitement level, we'll introduce another horse or two to the pasture, then add the canter, or ask kids to play volleyball nearby as we ride. Each time we add an exciting element, we go back to giving to the bit at the walk and improve performance there.

Calming down

Finally we can head back out to the trail. Or can we? The problem people have on the trail is that when horses get excited, they stay excited. We can't tell the horse not to get excited, but we can have a cue to tell him to calm down.

When a horse gets excited, his head comes up and his neck muscles stiffen. Well, we have a signal to get the neck muscles to relax and the jawbone to move to the side, so we'll use the same system to tell his head to go down.

We'll pick up one rein, as before, this time thinking about the horse's head going down. Look at the tip of the horse's ear as an indicator. When that ear goes down, instead of off to the side, we release the rein. The horse won't confuse the two signals (even though they may seem the same to you) because your two different thoughts will direct your body into slightly different postures. If you don't concentrate on the response you want, however, the horse will get confused.

Before too long, you'll develop a cue to tell the horse to drop his head and calm down.

Wrapping it up

So, now we have a plan to get our horse giving to the bit while walking, trotting and cantering smoothly, and we have a cue to tell him to calm down when he's excited. Without even working on it, we've trained our horse's emotions; he's in the habit of responding to our signals; and we have become better riders. We never once jerked on the reins or called our horse ugly names. We had fun with our dog and look forward to trail riding being fun again. ▣

Section III

Developing
Trailer-Loading Cues
and
Solving
Trailer-Loading Problems

15

Checking Out A Trailer

*After trailering horses thousands of miles and
seeing hundreds of other people's trailers,
John has developed some ideas about safety features
and convenience in trailers.*

Obviously you'll want a trailer that is safe, easy to haul, and easy to work around. We asked John to detail some features that he thinks are important in the choice of trailers.

Ramp or step-up

I definitely prefer a step-up trailer. Ramps are really for the convenience of owners, not horses. If you've taken the time to teach the horse to load and unload — one foot at a time — he won't worry about stepping up or down off the trailer. When you consider it, you are only asking him to step up a few inches — not even the height of his knee — which horses can do comfortably.

People think that a ramp is easier for the horse, but I find more possibilities for injury or upset to the horse on a ramp than a step, like backing off the side of the ramp, scaring himself. **A ramp on uneven ground will feel insecure to the horse. And, it puts the handler in an awkward position.** Ramps can get slippery when wet, especially with manure or in cold weather when they can get icy. Additionally, ramps are heavy, and you are carrying the weight of the ramp at the worst place to carry extra weight — the back of the trailer.

Most ramps have springs, but if they aren't working, the ramp is quite heavy to close. And most ramps come right up against the back doors so you're more likely to have rust problems there.

Ramps are more of a convenience for owners than horses.

Goose-neck or pull trailer

I prefer goosenecks because they are safer and easier to pull. With the ball close to the front of the towing vehicle, the balance is more stable. They don't have a tendency to move the vehicle around.

The turning radius of a gooseneck is shorter than for a pull trailer. You can turn a long gooseneck in a smaller space than you can a short pull trailer.

And, towing a pull trailer requires the tow vehicle to have at least an extra 20 percent towing capacity than to pull the same weight, same size gooseneck trailer. This makes a big difference if you live in mountainous areas or haul larger horses. In either event, you'll want to be sure you have enough towing capacity. It makes towing easier and the ride better.

Of course, though, an advantage to pull trailers is that you can put a camper shell on the pickup or pull it with a closed vehicle, like a Suburban, but then you'll have to think in terms of small trailers.

Axles

Always use at least two axles. Single-axle trailers, which are usually only found on home-made horse trailers, are dangerous, especially in case of a blow-out.

If you can, avoid leaf-spring axles. They are not as good as rubber-torsion bar axles — more problems with springs and connectors (hanging brackets) breaking. The rubber-torsion bar axles are better as far as maintenance and ride.

Center dividers

I prefer removable partitions over solid center dividers. They allow you to give a horse who scrambles more room. And, you can use them to haul furniture or equipment when you are not hauling horses. **Make sure that there are no projections — pins sticking up that the divider rests on, etc., that a horse could hurt himself on once the divider is out.**

Ideally, the center divider doesn't go all the way to the floor. That way the horse has a chance to spread out his feet for balance and lets air circulate better.

In slant-load trailers, I like stall partitions that are spring-loaded, so you can keep them out of the way until needed. Then a horse won't find himself bumping his chest into them when loading.

Flooring

If you have a wood floor, be sure to clean out the trailer after each use. Use a water sealer on the wood, and watch it closely. **Always use rubber mats over wood floors. They strengthen the floor, as well as protect the wood and help to cushion the ride.** I use shavings on top of the mats. It makes them less slick.

Take the mats out, wash them and let them dry after each use. If you are not going to use the trailer for several days, leave the mats out. Taking the mats in and out can be substantial work, so I prefer mats that are lighter in weight and can be cut into pieces of a size easy to manage.

Pull-type trailers require the tow vehicle to have more pulling capacity than do goose-necks.

Aluminum trailers usually have aluminum floors, which I would still cover with rubber mats.

If you are buying a second-hand trailer be sure to check the floor to see that it hasn't warped or rotted.

Other factors

■ Aluminum trailers are lighter than steel, which cuts down on your fuel economy and means you need more towing capacity than if you were towing an aluminum trailer. But aluminum trailers generally cost more. Aluminum trailers are about half to two-thirds the weight of steel, and they don't rust. Painted aluminum lasts longer than regular aluminum and requires less maintenance. (Aluminum should be acid washed regularly.)

■ Uninsulated trailers are hot in the summer and cold in the winter, so insulated trailers are preferred.

■ A white roof reflects sunlight.

■ If your tack compartment is in the rear of the trailer, it's ideal if you can fold it out of the way, because that makes the trailer more versatile. Then if you have to haul a garden tractor or something else that requires a wide-door opening, you aren't hampered by the tack compartment.

Rubber mats should be lightweight or cut into pieces that allow you to take them in and out of the trailer easily.

■ Stud doors on the side of four-horse trailers are great. They allow you to haul feed or equipment in a separate area from the horses, as well as their intended use.

■ I prefer a butt bar to a butt rope. Ropes can get up over the horse's back, giving him the idea it's time to back off the trailer. There are various types of butt bars, but they should give the horse a secure feeling when they are closed and be able to drop out of the way.

Butt ropes alone are not as secure as bars. The trailer on the left has a rope and a door to secure the horse. The trailer on the right has a padded bar.

■ When you are evaluating an older trailer, be sure to check for rust. Rust can cause big problems with the wiring, the floorboards, and so forth. Check also to be sure that the doors fit correctly. It's not uncommon to find warped doors that don't close correctly.

■ I don't like the term "escape" doors. Nobody should have to escape from a trailer. Escape implies there's a wreck going on. I'd rather think about having convenience doors than escape doors, so it's convenient to get in to check the horse or feed him. If we have to escape, we shouldn't be in there in the first place. Also, the more doors you put on a trailer, the more likelihood you have for moving parts to break or bend.

■ I'd prefer a feed manger to an open area and hay net. (I'm not a fan of nets.) People try to utilize that space under horse's head, and end up putting saddles or hay down there. It gets pretty sloppy. On the other hand, **it's nice to be able to let the horse's head down, especially on a long trip.** This helps prevent respiratory problems. Horses can also get a foot stuck over the chest bar if they rear.

If there are sharp edges around the feed manger area, that presents a potential problem for the horse getting injured.

A Breakaway "break" System, required by law in some states, is a safety feature you should not be without.

Side jacks and jacks that come up a little higher and out of the way are ideal.

■ The height of the trailer off the ground really only matters if you are going off the beaten path, where clearance is a factor. It's a less important factor going over the road.

■ The width of the trailer makes a big difference to some people. I'd rather have a seven- or eight-foot-wide trailer and have extra room inside. It means a narrower bumper over the wheel, but that's not a concern for me. Many people prefer a narrower trailer because it's easier to see around, but better mirrors may remedy their concern. In that case, you have a wider fender over the wheel, which is handy for sitting on at a horse show.

■ A double-jack system, with an identical jack on both sides, is ideal for a two-horse trailer. It's easier to level the front of the trailer. Also it's not uncommon for people using only one jack to forget to put it up, drive off and bend the jack. In that case, you'd have a spare.

■ On gooseneck trailers, it's a help if the jack is spring-loaded. It makes hooking up much easier.

■ Plexiglass windows sound like a good idea (and it's nice to have a lot of light in a trailer), but they don't open for ventilation.

■ I like to have a spare battery for the trailer so I can put the lights on when the trailer is not hooked to the pulling vehicle, or when I don't want to drain the truck battery.

The bottom edge of this trailer has a rubber bumper to protect the horse when he steps down.

If you have a rain gutter along the top of the trailer, you'll have less chance of water getting inside the windows.

Light switches accessible from outside the trailer are ideal, as well as having outside flood lights, plus the usual running and brake lights.

This is an efficient tack room in a converted stock trailer, with room for saddles, a tack trunk, feed, plus storage of small items on the door.

The convenience door on the front of this trailer lets in lots of air and light. However, the bar across the bottom is of a height where it would be easy for a horse to get his foot caught, or for a horse to step on the bar, bending it.

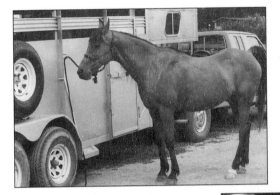

Watch out for sharp edges along the fender by the wheel. The edges should be rounded and ideally covered with rubber.

This little broken light cover is a sharp place a horse can cut himself.

Rust, rust, rust...

If the trailer is not cleaned out after use, urine and manure can rot the floor boards.

Single-jacks like this are prone to being bent easily. This is a new jack on an older trailer. Note the rust on the tongue area. Rust is a big concern on older trailers.

■ If you have a step-up trailer, the bottom edge of the step should be rounded or covered by a rubber bumper. When a horse steps off the trailer, often his hind foot is actually under the trailer for a moment, and the potential for him scraping himself on the step is strong if the edge is sharp.

Ventilation

Drop-down doors on both sides of the trailer let in light and ventilation. Little, old-fashioned windows are often not enough.

Screens or webbing at the windows let air in, but send a "don't touch" message to people who may want to pet or feed your horse while you are parked. It also prevents the horse from sticking his head out the window and rubbing his mane.

A recessed vent in the ceiling is ideal. That way you don't have any sharp edges. The vent should go both ways— let the heat out or fresh air in. If you close the trailer too tight, moisture builds up. That's when horses get respiratory problems. Instead, if you can open the vent backward, you let moisture out without letting wind in.

In cold weather, I put blankets on the horses but keep the air going through. I don't want to see a moisture buildup on the roof or the windows fogged up.

Stock-type trailers are fine, but it's nice to be able to completely close the trailer, including the back door, in case of bad weather or for warmth. ▣

Notes

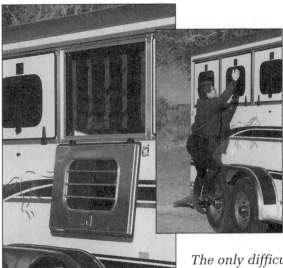

The only difficulty with drop-down doors is they may be hard to reach.

16

Trailer Loading 101

*One four-hour lesson can yield a lifetime of
safe and easy trailer loading.
Solve the trailer-loading blues once and for all.*

Trailer loading and unloading are two frustrating problems for both horses and owners. **Sure, there are lots of ways to load a horse, but simply getting the horse into the trailer isn't a suitable objective.**

It seems as if getting him into the trailer is the goal, until there's a problem with him racing backward to get out, hitting his head in the process, refusing to get out, kicking the trailer as you are trying to close the door, or refusing to get back into the trailer after the show or trail ride, after loading fine at home.

If you haven't specifically taught your horse to load, if it's just happened to work out OK so far, and if you think that using a butt rope on occasion isn't much of a bother, one of these days you'll likely encounter a problem.

Our goal, you see, goes beyond just getting him in. **We want him to go into the trailer every time, ride quietly and unload under any circumstance.** Also, we want to be able to load him ourselves, without extra hands to push or to hold ropes, without our having to get in the trailer with him, and of course, without injury to us or the horse. A tall order, but it can be done in just four hours, all at once or in segments, whichever is more convenient for you.

We'll begin our trailer-loading lessons away from the trailer, so that neither you nor the horse gets too anxious about the trailer. This is also a way that folks without a trailer can teach their horse trailer-loading skills. And, if your horse already rides in the trailer, particularly if he's not a problem loader but you want to make sure he knows the lesson, you'll be practicing skills that will apply to lots of different circumstances, not just trailer loading.

Anything we want our horse to do consistently requires teaching him a cue. We're going to use the "go forward" cue to ask him to take a step forward, the same cue we used to teach the horse to go forward on the lunge line. **The concept is that we will irritate or "bug" the horse and immediately stop bugging him when he's done what we want him to do.** In this case, we want him to move one of his feet forward.

The lesson

Stand facing the horse's left shoulder, left hand holding the lead rope about two inches below the snap, right hand holding a stiff buggy or dressage whip. **Your left hand is just to help guide the horse's head forward, so he doesn't turn it to one side or the other.** It's not to lead or pull him forward; this is a rear-wheel-drive operation.

Begin tapping the top of the horse's left hip with the end of the whip. You are going to tap only hard enough to irritate him. There are several reasons for this:

1. You want him to respond to a light signal; you are not hitting him to get him into the trailer.

2. Should you need to make your signal more intense, you don't want to end up beating on him.

3. The most important reason is that once you've hit a horse, he's learned that hitting him isn't going to kill him, so hitting won't work.

Whenever you use pain to motivate a horse, you'll eventually have to use more pain to get the same level of motivation as you did initially, and we've all seen where that leads. So, we don't want to cause the horse pain. We want him to feel "bugged."

In this case, stopping the tapping is like giving him a pay check. It's what he'll work for. It operates like the release does in the "giving to the bit" lessons. **The tap is a cue, and when the horse does what we want, we release him from the cue.**

Let the taps begin

Begin tapping. When he moves something forward, immediately stop tapping, then pet him. I say, something, because this requires a judgment call on the part of the trainer.

We use a specific spot on the horse's hip to tell him to go forward, just as you use specific button on the remote to turn on the TV.

Ideally, you will keep tapping until he moves one of his feet forward. But, should he stand there a long time, you may want to find a reason to stop tapping (and relieve your tired arm). In that case, stop tapping if the horse leans forward, or cocks one of his feet like he might take a step, or even if you can read that he's thinking about taking a step forward.

If you have to settle for something less than a step forward, don't be discouraged. Your horse has actually given you the opportunity to put one additional step into the teaching/learning process. The more steps you have in the process, the more secure the lesson will be.

Repeat this exercise until you can tap the horse's hip and have him step forward right away. You'll want to control his movement so that he takes only one step or so at a time. When you can do this consistently, ask him to go forward in a more confined area.

When the horse goes forward consistently from both sides, out in an open area, you are ready for the next step. Put two railroad ties or jump poles on the ground about three feet apart, and ask the horse to step "into" the hallway you have created for him. "Load" one foot, then unload it. When he goes forward into the space, ask for two feet in, then back his two feet out. Move on to three feet, then

In this sequence of photos, John is teaching Seattle to step up onto a big log. Positioning himself carefully (so if the log moves, John won't be hurt by the log or Seattle), he asks Seattle to go forward.

Seattle tries various options — he steps over the log, he paws the log, and he even changes feet. He steps around the log. He doesn't have a clue what John wants of him. By John's keeping the cue the same and the horse's nose in the same spot, Seattle eventually is able to figure out what option John wants.

John is asking Seattle to step across the railroad ties, in effect "loading" him into the grass on the other side of the tie. At this stage of the lesson, Seattle is learning how the "go forward" cue works, while gaining confidence in John's consistent, specific directions.

four, each time asking the horse to stand for a few moments before you back him out, so he doesn't think you are asking for the complete sequence of two steps forward and two steps back. **Remember, the objective is to control each step the horse makes.**

Next, apply this same lesson to asking the horse to step into the washrack or into a stall, loading one foot and unloading, and so forth. By now, the lesson should have started to become fun.

Once you've mastered asking him to go forward, you'll want to work with asking him to step *up*. This takes a little creativity. You might stand railroad ties so they are the height of a trailer, or just a little higher. Or, maybe you can use steps or a trail bridge. Some people have even built a platform specifically for teaching this and other leading lessons to their horses.

But, before you ask your horse to step up onto something strange, ask yourself, "Can the horse get hurt doing this?" or, "If the object moves, can the horse get hurt?" If the answer is yes, then don't use that object. But if there's no risk of injury to horse or handler, use the "go forward" cue to ask the horse to put one foot onto the step or platform. Of course, when he does, immediately stop tapping and pet him.

IT SEEMS AS IF GETTING THE HORSE INTO THE TRAILER IS THE GOAL, UNTIL THERE'S A PROBLEM WITH HIM RACING BACKWARD TO GET OUT.

If he's reluctant, don't make a big deal about it, just gently tap until he looks at the platform or paws at it. **Here's when you might consider rewarding his forward *thought* by stopping the taps, so he knows he's on the right track.** If he paws at it with one foot, stop tapping and praise him. Do this until every time you tap him he paws the platform. Then tap until he steps on the platform instead of just pawing (he'll probably leave his foot on the platform following one of the pawings).

So now, your tap has changed the cue from meaning "move something forward" to "paw with one foot" to "step forward with one foot," because your stopping the taps tells the horse he guessed correctly.

"Load" one foot onto the platform. Then, putting a little backward pressure on the lead rope, ask him to "unload" that foot. Praise him and repeat this lots of times with one foot. Then "load" two feet onto the platform, pet him and let him stand there for a moment, then unload two feet and praise him. Then three feet, then four.

John uses the trailer ramp to teach Seattle to step one foot on, then off, and so forth until the whole horse is "loaded" across the ramp, stands quietly, then moves forward off the ramp again at John's "go forward" request.

Notice that when John asked Seattle to step off the ramp, he did not step away from the trailer and lead Seattle's head. He used the "go forward" cue, and Seattle's back feet moved his body forward.

Use your imagination to see what is around the barn that you can use to teach this lesson. Perhaps have the horse step onto a tarp, or "load" him in and out of the barn, or have him step onto the concrete and back "off" onto the grass. You'll find that while preparing your horse for trailer loading, his leading-manners will improve.

Ready for the trailer

By now, trailer loading should be a cinch. Put the trailer on level ground in a secure location, like inside a big field or arena, and hooked up to your truck. Close the front doors, feed room doors and escape hatch up front. **Do not put feed in the trailer or on the floor**

of the trailer. Open the back doors on the right side of the trailer, but leave the left side closed. You are going to stand outside the left door; at no point are you going to step inside the trailer or "lead" the horse into the trailer. You want him to go past you and into the trailer by himself.

Lead your horse up to the back of the trailer and just pet him and let him stand there. As you approach the trailer, there may be a point at which the horse stops. That's his safe zone. Let him stand there and relax. Then use the "go forward" cue to ask him to move one of his feet forward. Do this until you are at the trailer, then proceed through the stepping in and out of each foot as we described earlier.

When you are ready, face his left shoulder as you've been doing all along for the "go forward" cue. Your left hand will keep his head facing forward, and your right hand will do the tapping. It's important to keep his nose facing into the trailer. Don't turn him away or allow him to turn away.

He knows the routine by now. Do exactly as you did with the platform. When he moves one of his feet forward, immediately stop tapping and praise him. **Do not ask him or allow him to walk right into the trailer. Remember, the objective is to teach him to load so he'll load anytime, and that requires loading and unloading him under control.**

Load and unload the first foot 200 times (count them). Now go on to the second foot. Load one foot, then ask him with your taps to go forward again. Keep tapping until he moves his second foot forward. If he doesn't step onto the ramp or up into the trailer but just lifts the foot, accept that at first. Stop tapping and praise him. Build on that until the horse puts both front feet in the trailer and stands there. Then, load and unload the first and second front feet 200 times.

Be careful not to reverse the cue

About this time (you may have already experienced it at the platform stage), if the horse steps backward — and you stop tapping — you will have reversed the cue. Remember when we were working with the platform and we changed the tapping cue from meaning "move something" to "move one foot forward"? **Well, if you stop tapping as the horse backs up, you'll teach him that tapping means "back up," which will really confuse both of you.** If he backs up at any point in this whole operation, move with him and continue to tap.

When this happens, I maintain the same amount of pressure that

I had on the lead rope when the horse was standing there. **I don't try to stop his backward motion by the lead rope, although it feels like the natural thing to do.** And I don't add any pressure on the lead rope because I don't want to cause the horse to rear or pull back hard. My feet move at the same or a slightly faster speed than the horse's, because I'm trying to stay with his hindquarters in order to keep tapping. The backing-up stage doesn't happen with every horse, but should it happen, you'll be prepared to do the right thing.

Now that you've loaded two feet, ask for the third. Allow the horse plenty of time to relax before you ask him to back out. But, if he steps up and backs right out on his own, don't panic. Just take your time and play the minute game. Load and unload three feet 100 times.

Next, ask the horse to go forward again and load his fourth foot. Let him pause inside the trailer, then ask him to step down and back out of the trailer. If he's been in and out of the trailer 500 times already, stepping up with the fourth foot, then backing out, should not be too traumatic.

The cue to back out

You do not want the horse to decide when it's time to come out of the trailer. Everything we do with our horses has them under control, so that we don't risk injury to people or other horses.

A lot of times horses will go in for a second, then come right back out. But you want to give the horse a cue to come out of the trailer *before* he comes out on his own. When you sense he's going to come out in two seconds, pick up the lead rope and ask him to come out in one. **If he knows you'll cue him, instead of backing out on his own, he'll start to wait longer and longer for the cue.**

The cue I use to ask a horse to back up is just a little backward pressure on the lead rope. Don't pull the horse's head back; just take the slack out of the rope and wait for the horse to take a step backward. That will release pressure from the lead rope.

Loaded up, now what?

You are almost done. Once your horse stands perfectly still in the trailer for long enough that you think it is safe, drape the lead rope over his back, close the butt bar and back door. *Then,* go around to the front of the trailer and take the lead rope off the horse or tie his

❶ *When John is ready to teach Seattle to load into the trailer, he parks the trailer on level ground and closes the left back door.*
❷ *It doesn't matter that Seattle is not facing directly into the trailer but has swung his rear end nearly out of reach of John's tap. John doesn't vary the cue but keeps Seattle's nose pointed where he wants him to go. Because he's been taught the "go forward" cue in so many forms already, Seattle knows John will be persistent with the "go forward" signal and that he'll have to make a movement.*

❸ *Eventually Seattle moves himself forward, and his body follows where his nose pointed. When he stands quietly with two feet in the trailer, John just praises him and lets him rest there.*

❹ *John asks Seattle to back his two front feet out of the trailer. This is as valuable for teaching the horse to unload confidently as it is for loading.*

❺ *John again uses the "go forward" cue to ask Seattle to step his third foot into the trailer, then asks him to step back out again. He does this 100 times. Then he asks Seattle to*

step up into the trailer with all four feet and back all the way out again, 100 times. At the end of the exercise, Seattle will have stepped into the trailer and backed out of the trailer, in one form or another, 600 times.

head forward. **BUT, never tie a horse in a trailer if he has not been taught to stand tied.**

You are ready for the road. Make sure you are comfortable driving your rig before you load the horse. Take him on a short ride, making sure to take the corners easily and brake slowly, so the horse learns to keep his balance — then return home.

Allow him to stand in the trailer for a few minutes before you take him out so he doesn't get the idea that he has to jump out the moment the truck stops. Then, take him with you on errands the following week, to the bank, the grocery store and so forth. Just be sure, that when you park the air vents are open, so he gets plenty of air and the trailer doesn't get too hot.

What if you are in a hurry?

It's best never to be in a hurry when you are working with a horse. The more excited and intense you are, the less likely you will be able to communicate to your horse in a way that makes sense to him.

Nevertheless, there are times when you don't have a full four hours to teach this lesson. Where can you legitimately cut corners? **Going forward on cue is non-negotiable.** If you are pressed for time, assuming that the horse is reasonably well halter-broken, you can eliminate the "loading" between poles, or onto a tarp or the bridge, and use the "go forward" cue at or near the back of the trailer. However, by eliminating those steps, you may encounter more resistance from the horse.

Secondly, you can cut down on the number of times you have the horse go in and out of the trailer; but, after you've worked through this with a horse or two, you'll realize that 100 times does not really take very much time, and the added safety factor is worth the time spent.

The rule for tying

There's nothing more dangerous than having a wreck in an enclosed space. In fact, the rule of thumb that I use is, "If I don't have to tie, I don't." If I don't have a particular reason to tie the horse up, such as him biting another horse, or moving around in the trailer, then I don't tie him. If a horse puts his head down in the trailer, he'll learn to bring it back up and travel with it up. PH

17

Eliminating Escape Options

*Sometimes while working on trailer loading,
horses look for options other than going forward.
We'll show you how to fine-tune trailer loading
and how to improve your horse's
ground-handling manners in the process.*

Many of us take for granted that we can open the back door of a trailer and have our horse walk right in. Not only is it great not to have to fight about the trailer, but you have a sense of partnership — that the horse is enjoying his job as much as you are.

Most horses that don't go in the trailer well also don't lead as well as we'd like them to. **We consider trailer loading advanced leading work, and that's hard for horses who don't have a good leading foundation.** As you work through the exercises in this article, you'll be improving your horse's responsiveness to you going forward, stopping, turning and softening his neck, and you'll be establishing the habit of cooperation. You'll see improvement not just in his trailer loading, but in all areas of leading as well.

If we want the horse to walk into the trailer without our having gone into the trailer ahead of him, he has to walk past us. But, what if, despite the fact you've taught the "Trailer Loading 101" lesson, your horse tries escape options at the trailer?

When we first use the "go forward" cue, the horse gets irritated at the tapping on him and he moves, generally in the direction we have his nose pointed. Once we stop tapping, the horse is left with the job of figuring out why we tapped and what, if anything, he may have done to get us to stop tapping. After repetition and experimentation, the horse figures out that it's movement we want.

Sometimes the horse is actually cooperating with us, but it seems like he's being disobedient. For instance, if I positioned a horse with his nose to a wall and asked him to go forward, he'd say, "John, I can't go forward into the wall. I'll have to crowd between you and the wall, or I'll have to back up, or move some other direction if you insist that I move." Well, that's what the horse may feel like when he is at the trailer and you ask him to go forward. You know you want him to step into the trailer, but he may not see that as an option, so he's forced to look for other ways to respond to your signal.

The horse's fear level also factors in, perhaps fear of the trailer itself, perhaps fear from a previous incident, perhaps because traditionally when people decide it's time to get their horse into a trailer they become pretty intense, and the horse actually becomes afraid of what the person may do. Add to fear the fact you are teaching the horse something new, which may also be new to you, and we have a set-up in which the horse may say, "I don't want to play this game anymore."

Now you see why establishing a pattern of asking the horse to do something easy, then rewarding him when he does it, is so important. **By the time he gets to the potentially scary place (the trailer), he will be in the habit of cooperating, and you will have established a language that tells him you expect him to obey, but that you won't ask him to do anything that is too hard for him.**

Most trailer-loading problems are related to leading problems. Working the length of a tarp helps develop control.

The horse who has been taught the go forward cue and asked to step onto a variety of platforms will understand the "go forward" cue at the trailer easily.

Once the horse knows the gist of what we want, he'll go through learning cycles. His performance will start off bad, then get good, then get worse, and he'll try every option he knows. Then he will get better for a short time, then bad again — but not very bad or for very long. Finally, he'll be good consistently, at which time we'll say that he's learned the lesson.

Don't be discouraged if the horse seems to know something at one time, then acts like he doesn't have a clue the next. Just work with him, getting him consistent at each stage, and he'll know the lesson for life.

Also remember that you are the teacher — teaching the student a new lesson. **The right answer is always clearer to the teacher than the student, so there's no cause for the teacher getting upset with the student.** A cool head and a persistent cue will pay off.

Common problems

■ **The horse moves backward instead of forward.**
If the horse moves backward, apply the "go forward" cue, making the taps firmer until he takes a step forward. Don't pull on his head, just move with him, tapping. Keep tapping, even if the horse backs 80 feet from the trailer. The moment he makes a step forward, stop tapping. Pet him, walk him back up to the trailer and start again. The mistake most people make is they stop tapping as the horse begins to back. If they do that, the horse learns that the tap means to back up.

■ **The horse goes forward when I tell him, but then walks in circles around me. I can't get him to stop.**

When you want the horse to stop, put tension on the lead rope — just a signal so he doesn't feel totally free to keep walking. He has to do the stopping; you can't make him stop. At some point, he'll at least slow his feet, pausing. Release the lead rope and pet him. When he's consistently slowing in response to the lead rope, then you'll hold the lead rope until he stops his feet, not just slows them. When he consistently stops his feet in response to light tension on the lead rope, hold the rope until he stops his feet, brings his nose slightly toward you and relaxes the muscles of his neck. Do this until every time you ask him to stop, he stops with his neck relaxed.

■ **The horse stops before we get to the trailer.**

Let's say that you are 15 feet from the trailer when the horse stops. This is the spot where the horse feels safe and you have control. Let him just stand there and pet him for a few minutes; do not ask him to go forward immediately. You are telling him that there is a place where he can be safe, that you are not going to pick on him, that he's going to be just fine. The longer you wait there, the more secure he will feel. This will save you time in the long run.

Throughout the lesson, from here all the way to the feed manger, you'll be stopping him and asking him to stand calmly. When the horse gets excited at a point later in the training, the longer you waited in his "feel-safe" zone, the easier it will be to calm him down again and get him back to this spot. For instance, let's say at some point in the training, the horse backs 20 feet from the trailer. He'll remember that at 15 feet, he could stand without your pressuring him, so that time at 15 feet will pay off.

When the horse is relaxed, work in this location, asking the horse to take one step forward. Then stop him and pet him. Continue one step or a few steps at a time, asking him to step toward the trailer. Remind yourself that you are not interested in getting the horse into the trailer yet. You are interested in getting control of the horse's movements and in having him feel secure.

■ **The horse crowds me or pushes past me, knocking into me.**

If the horse crowds a bit when you are working on the leading lessons before you get to the trailer, then you can ask him to bring his nose slightly down and toward you, relaxing his neck as if you were asking him to stop; then move his shoulders over away from you, asking him to step slightly to the right.

If the horse pulls back on the lead, you can send him away, then pull him toward you. That will teach him to "give" to the pressure on the line.

This crowding behavior is an indicator that this horse will most likely try to shove himself between you and the trailer when you go to load him. When that happens, instead of creating a fight, step out of his way, but begin tapping his front legs with the whip (below the knee) the whole time he's walking forward. The moment he takes a step backward, stop tapping and pet him. Let him settle down, then start toward the trailer again.

If this happens at the trailer, it is especially important that you step aside, out of the horse's way, until his back end has cleared the trailer. You don't want to risk him banging into the trailer, perhaps injuring himself in the process. Don't try to forcibly stop his forward motion by pulling on the halter or by shoving the horse's chest or shoulder.

After several attempts, when the horse begins to crowd you and you position your whip, he'll back off.

■ **The horse tries to bring his head over mine, invading my space.** When this happens, it is usually at the trailer. Instead of pulling away from you or trying to fit himself between you and the trailer, the horse just raises his head and pushes his chest into where you are standing. You'll want to control his nose; don't fight the whole horse. Just raise the whip (you don't usually have to touch him with it), and he'll pull his head backward. Then step toward his nose, asking him to back up a step.

■ **The horse swings his hindquarters away from me, making them parallel with the trailer.**

Don't worry about that for now; don't let yourself become distracted about the hind end. All you really have to do is control the nose of the horse. If you can teach the horse's nose to go into the trailer all the way up to the feed manger, you won't have to worry about where his hind end is.

Once you've headed the horse's nose to the trailer with the intent to load him, keep his nose pointed into the trailer. Don't circle him around if he gets out of position, and don't lead him away to get a better approach.

■ **The horse swings his hindquarters toward me, pushing me toward the trailer door.**

Be sure to keep his nose pointed either directly into the trailer, or bring it toward you, and keep yourself out of the way of his hindquarters. As he brings his hindquarters toward you, tap his hip firmly until he stops moving his hind end toward you. Do that each time he begins to bring his hindquarters over, and he'll learn to keep them away from you.

■ **The horse stiffens his neck and looks away from me.**

If the horse does this while you are working away from the trailer, it's a pretty good indication that at some time he'll try to pull away from you or drag you off. Work on leading exercises, making sure that the horse's nose is slightly turned toward you. Each time you stop him, keep tension on the rope until his nose looks toward you and his neck muscles soften. If he is looks to the right, he's thinking of moving to the right. You will want to change his pattern of thinking, quickly.

If the horse is not just stiffening his neck, but actually showing signs of pulling away, you'll want to teach him the "come here" cue. Send him two or three feet away from you, then put tension on the lead line, asking him to come toward you. As soon as he steps toward you, release the tension. When he begins to get the idea, send him away more vigorously, which increases his emotion level, then ask him to come back.

If the horse is particularly strong in his attempt to pull away, or if you are loading him in an area that is not enclosed, such as after

As you teach your horse to load, you are also teaching him to unload. Repetition is the key to helping the horse feel safe and to minimizing his fear once the trailer starts moving.

a trail ride, put a full cheek snaffle bridle on him instead of the halter. Attach the lead rope to the bit ring closest to you. Don't jerk on the bit (any more than you should jerk on the halter), but it will give you more control. Be quick to release the tension on the lead rope as soon as the horse does what you want him to do. The quicker you tell him he did the right thing, the more consistently he'll do what you ask.

■ **The horse rears.**

Take care to be in a safe position, so the horse doesn't strike you with one of his feet, hit his legs below the knees with the dressage whip the whole time his legs are in the air. The moment one foot touches the ground, stop hitting him. Be sure you are hitting below the knee — you don't want to ever hit a horse above the knee — that will just make him want to rear more. This technique works as well for horses wearing protective boots as without. Just hit the boots the whole time the horse in the air.

■ **The horse bites.**

Biting is the most dangerous thing a horse can do. If the horse has a history of biting, or you think he might bite, put a muzzle on him. If he actually bites at you, he's declared war. You have to let him think he's going to die — and you have only three seconds in which to do it.

Hit him (below the withers only), jump at him, scream at him — whatever you can do to let him know he's just made the worst mistake of his life. **Do not,** under any circumstances, hit the horse around the head or flip the lead rope at him in such a way that the end could hit him around the head. You don't want to risk having the horse's eye injured or the horse injured in any way. You want to give him a scare. At the end of three seconds, cease activity and go back to the lesson. Pet him.

■ **The horse responds away from the trailer but not at the trailer.**
This is going to happen. Anything we want the horse to do, we have to teach him in a low-threat situation — and train him beyond responsiveness in that unemotional setting — so that when his emotions are running high he will still respond to the cue. When he's not responding as we want him to, we need to know which cue he's not responding to and how to get him to respond. Know the options in advance and what to do when he tries each one of them.

■ **The horse kicks at the whip.**
One of the reasons that we tap the horse high on the hip, instead of lower down, is so we don't elicit a kicking response. But if the horse kicks out, most of the time if you ignore it the behavior goes away. Don't make a big deal about it.

If he becomes preoccupied with kicking out at the whip, maybe kicking 50 times, then go one for one. If he kicks out at the whip, hit him once, fairly hard, below his hocks. Several times like that and he usually stops kicking.

■ **The horse goes up to the trailer fine, but then won't move a foot forward, even if I've been tapping for quite awhile.**
Time your tapping when you think the horse may be thinking about moving forward. If you tap when there's no chance of getting movement, you are defeating your purpose. But be careful, once you've started tapping, not to stop tapping before the horse does something that you want him to do. Otherwise you'll teach him, "When I tap, the thing I want you to do is just stand still." You may have to settle for less movement than you had in mind, such as his dropping his head, but don't stop tapping until you get some forward movement.

When the horse's front feet are at the trailer, you are going to concentrate on asking the back feet to move forward. His back feet are going to load his front feet.

When you tap and the horse cocks one back foot, stop tapping. Build on that, until the horse cocks that hind foot each time you tap.

The more time you take at this step, the less likely the horse will get upset further in the process. When he's consistently cocking his foot in response to the tap, then tap again, stopping the taps when the horse brings his hind foot forward.

Follow the same pattern working with the other hind foot. Most horses will bring one front foot forward before both hind legs are too far forward; but if not, the horse's muscles will tire and eventually prompt him to move. Be sure to stop the taps and pet the horse when he moves in the right direction, but don't allow backward movement.

The minute game

You can use this game with the whole horse in the trailer, or at any point along the way. Start with the horse out of the trailer for 60 seconds. Then put him in the trailer for two seconds, which means he's out for 58 seconds. Then have him in the trailer for four seconds, and out for 56, then in for six seconds and out for 54, and so forth. If you combine the minute game with teaching the horse to wait for a cue, the horse will learn to stay in the trailer until you ask him to back out. ■PH■

Notes

18

Trailering Dilemmas

Trailering 101 is completed,
and your horse loads easily, but then
problems develop. That's when
our frustration peaks, and we need a plan.

Question. *My horse loads fine at home, but when we are ready to come home after a day of showing, he won't get in.*

Answer. That's not an uncommon problem, and the solution is easy. In order for him to obey your cue when he's excited, you'll have to train your horse beyond the level of responsiveness you need at home.

Practice loading him several times when everything is quiet, then introduce a little commotion — park the trailer in an unusual spot, for instance, maybe out in a pasture or halfway down the driveway. When he loads and unloads calmly and consistently with that level of excitement or new location, have someone ride near the trailer, first at the walk, later at a canter. Then load another horse with your horse, load and unload in other locations, such as at a neighbor's farm, and so forth. **The idea is to stimulate him a little bit, but not so much that he can't concentrate on what you are asking him. Build on your earlier success.**

Q. *When I tap the horse's hip, sometimes he moves forward and sometimes backward.*

A. That tells you that the horse understands the cue means "move something," but he doesn't understand it as "move forward." If he backs up, continue tapping. In fact, make your taps harder, stopping tapping the moment that he steps forward again. If you stop tapping

185

as he's backing up, you've reversed the cue and taught him that the tap means "go backward."

Q. *My horse stands with two feet in the trailer and his hind feet firmly planted outside the trailer.*

A. Work on your cue to go forward while the horse has two feet in the trailer. The taps should get firmer and quicker until you get some forward movement.

It's a judgment call as to when to tap — only tap when you think you have a good chance of getting forward motion. If you don't think the horse is ready, wait. I wouldn't tap on the horse if I thought he was going to back up. I'd let him stand there. The longer I wait, the more comfortable the horse is with two feet in the trailer, and the more tired his hind legs are getting. So waiting isn't bad.

Q. *My horse goes into the trailer just fine. But, he zooms out of the trailer, sometimes hitting his head in the process.*

A. Teach him to load and unload one foot at a time. By loading one foot 200 times, we are also unloading it 200 times. **This gives the**

horse confidence that he'll be able to find his footing when he backs out. As you load and unload the back feet, he'll stand for short periods with two feet in the trailer and two feet out. He'll figure out his balance and that he doesn't have to rush out.

If you are thorough in teaching the trailer-loading lessons, your horse will back out of the trailer as calmly as he steps into it.

Q. *My horse goes part of the way in, but comes right back out.*

A. In this case, play the "minute game." Start with the horse outside the trailer for 60 seconds. Then put him in the trailer for two seconds, ask him to back out calmly, then stand outside the trailer for 58 seconds. Then four seconds in and 56 out, eight seconds in and 52 out, and so forth. Pretty soon he'll be standing there a full minute, then two minutes ...

The other thing you'll want to do is give the horse a cue to come out. **If you give him a cue, instead of just letting him back out on his own, he'll wait longer and longer for the cue.** If you think he's going to come out in two seconds, then ask him to come out in one second. Play both the minute game and the cue-to-come-out, and your horse will learn to stay in the trailer until you invite him to step out.

Q. *My horse backs out just as you close the butt bar.*

A. Use the "go forward" cue to tell him to step forward. We can use the cue inside the trailer as well as outside.

Play the minute game and make sure the horse feels safe inside the trailer. Go around and bang the doors and sides of the trailer so he learns to stand inside despite the noises. **If he tries to back out, tap him, making the taps harder until he takes a step forward.** Be sure you don't close the door or raise the butt bar until he stands with all the noise going on.

Q. *My horse tries to turn around in the trailer.*

A. If a horse is trying to turn around in a two-horse trailer, he's probably gone through the trailer-loading lesson too fast and did not back out enough times. So he doesn't know how to back out, or he's not sure about it. Just go back to square one, teaching him to load and unload each foot.

Q. *What about the horse who jumps in the manger?*

A. A horse who jumps into the manger almost always has had his head tied in the trailer. He panics, as if someone was holding his head under water, and comes up and strikes at what he thinks has his head — and ends up with his front feet in the feed manger. **This often happens if the horse's head is tied before the butt bar or trailer door is closed.**

The horse who has a tendency to scramble, or get upset in the trailer, should have plenty of time to look around and get secure in his environment. Remove the center divider, then ask the horse to step into the trailer. If he decides to turn around, that's fine. Just reassure him and let him stand in the trailer for a while. You can even bang the doors and rattle the butt chain so that he gets used to noises and vibrations. Then calmly ask the horse to step out of the trailer.

When that happens, leave him alone until he's settled down. Both you and the horse are in a dangerous situation. There's going to be a lot of pressure on the horse's head from the tie rope. The horse is likely to continue to strike and thrash about. If you open the feed manger door to get the horse undone, the horse could strike and crush your hand. And as you untie the rope, you can end up catching your hand or fingers in the loop and lose fingers. **So, be extremely cautious and don't do anything fast.** When the noise dies down, peek into the trailer and try to figure out what is the best way to get the horse untied or the rope cut.

Leaving a horse's head free (not tied) will not guarantee that he won't end up in the manger. He can still jump and get his feet in the manger; however, he's less likely to do so and can get himself out of the manger much easier than if he's tied.

If the horse has a history of jumping into the manger, even if he loads into the trailer fine, go back to the beginning, working him through the loading and unloading steps, and do not tie his head when he's in the trailer. It will take many repetitions for the horse to learn that he doesn't have to panic.

Q. *When do you tie the horse's head?*

A. If I don't have a particular reason to tie him, such as to prevent him from biting another horse, or moving around in the trailer, then I don't tie him. If the horse puts his head down in the trailer, he'll learn to bring it back up and travel with it up.

I think it's healthy for the horse to be able to get his head down while he's going down the road. It lets him clear his sinuses and his nose, so he's less likely to get sick if he can blow his nose when he's in the trailer.

Never, never, never tie a horse in a trailer who hasn't learned to stand tied, otherwise you'll have a wreck in an enclosed space, and the horse is likely to get hurt.

Also, even with horses that will stand tied, if I have any doubts at all about the horse — that he might get scared — and for some reason I have to tie his head, then I'll close the butt bar and back door before I tie the horse.

Q. *What should I do if my horse throws a fit in the trailer?*

A. Stand back, wait for all the noise to stop, then sneak up on the trailer. You can't do much while he's fighting it, and keeping yourself and other people safe is most important.

The first thing to do in any wreck, not just this wreck, is stand still. It's not our normal reaction, but it's the correct one. What's normal is to rush over and try to help the horse, but in many cases it only causes the horse to panic more, and it puts both the person and the horse in danger.

Once it's quiet, try to make a logical decision about what is the best way to approach the horse so no one gets hurt and the horse can be helped. Slowly approach the trailer to see what kind of predicament the horse is in. Then stop and think about what would be the safest way to help the horse.

Q. *Do you recommend protective gear when teaching your horse to load in the trailer?*

A. Any time there is even a vague possibility of injury, it's a good idea to protect both him and yourself. Boots or bandages protect the horse's legs, and a head bumper or "crash helmet" protects the top of his head.

For you, it's not a bad idea to wear gloves, especially if you think he may pull away. Of course, never loop a lead line in a way that it could tighten around your hand.

You might wear a helmet if you think he may rear or strike. Again, if you've done sufficient preparation — teaching your horse the cue before coming near the trailer — both you and he will be much safer.

Q. *What do you do about the horse who paws in the trailer?*

A. First, make sure he's been taught to stand tied — that he has learned to give to pressure on the lead rope. Then, have him practice standing tied outside the trailer first for hours at a time, and in different places where he can stand tied for three to four hours a day on multiple days, making sure he's not in the hot sun. (Frequently, the horse who paws in the trailer also has a hard time standing without pawing in other locations.)

Then tie him to the outside of the trailer, to the back of the trailer, then inside the trailer. Then take him on short trips when you do errands in town, such as going to the bank or grocery store. Make sure the vents are left open so he has plenty of air when he's stands in the trailer while you are shopping.

Don't yell at him, and don't correct him. **Never scold a horse while he's tied or in a trailer. It can lead to other problems, such as pulling back or getting scared in the trailer.**

If you are worried about damage to the trailer or floor boards from

Teaching a horse to stand tied outside the trailer without pawing is the first step to teaching him to stand inside without pawing.

his pawing, you can put an extra rubber mat on the floor or mount plywood on the trailer in front of him.

Many times the horse rides along fine, then when the trailer stops or when the horse has been in the parked trailer awhile, he begins to paw. Don't pay him attention every time he paws.

What usually happens is that if the horse gets some attention, the time intervals between his demands get shorter. If he started pawing in four minutes, pretty soon he's pawing in three, then one, then as soon as you stop the trailer, even at a stoplight — the horse thinks he's going to get out or get some kind of attention, even if it's just a person yelling at him. It becomes a conditioned response — the horse trains the person to come get him out or to notice him.

You want to reverse that process. **Only give him attention when he's standing quietly, and don't take him out while he's pawing.**

Q. *What do you do about the horse who won't haul alone?*

A. Teach him to load in the trailer as we've discussed, then he should be safe in the trailer. Beyond that, start taking him on short trips.

On the other hand, if you have two horses to haul who don't get along, you can work up to putting them together. Put the two horses that you want to trailer in pens with a center fence dividing them, feeding them in areas separated by some distance. As days go by, move the feed until you have it on the ground between them, so they eat together.

When that is accomplished, begin tying them to the fence, at first a distance from each other, but both facing the same direction. Then move them closer until they can stand tied, side by side, separated only by the fence panel.

Q. *What about the horse who scrambles in the trailer?*

A. Scrambling is a fear-related problem; the horse feels as if he can't stand up. It's a combination of claustrophobia and an equilibrium problem. While it's serious, it is easy to solve. **When a horse scrambles, it's usually against the outside wall of the trailer, so the first thing we'll do is to take the center partition out of the trailer.**

When you put the horse in the trailer, tie him up, but tie him longer than you normally would — long enough that he can get his nose about 6 to 12 inches behind the chest bar or feed manger. (This, of course, presumes that he has been trained to stand tied.)

Take him to an open field or parking lot. Drive carefully, making turns at about 5 or 10 miles per hour. Do this for about 30 minutes.

Then take a lead rope and tie it where the center partition would go, about flank high. Stretch it tight. That will cause the horse to stand on his side of the trailer, but the lead rope won't give him enough support that he can lean up against it. (He has to lean up against something in order to be able to scramble.)

Drive him around another 30 minutes that way, increasing speed but still driving carefully. Then put another horse in the trailer with him, one who doesn't scramble or push.

Don't put the center partition back in the trailer for at least six months, and practice driving the horse around at least once a week, either by himself or with another horse. After the lead-rope work, the horse should at least be able to travel safely by himself.

Be cautious about putting other horses in the trailer. The scrambler can lean against the other horse. If the first work isn't done thoroughly, you can end up with both horses fearful and scrambling.

When working with a horse who scrambles in the trailer, replace the center divider with a taut rope so that he doesn't have anything to brace against. The solution to a scrambling problem is not complicated, but it takes repeated sessions before a horse is comfortable.

Q. *What do you do if a horse is "stuck" inside the trailer and won't back out?*

A. Generally this happens in a two-horse trailer, because the horse hasn't learned to back out on cue, one foot at a time. **The ultimate solution is to retrain him to load into the trailer, because that also trains him to unload at the same time.**

But, if the horse is already stuck in the trailer, pick up on the lead rope while you are standing on one side of the partition and the horse is on the other. Put just enough pressure on the rope to have the horse bend his nose two inches back, asking him to flex at the poll. Hold that pressure until the horse takes a two-inch step backward. When he does, release the line, let him have his nose in a normal position and pet him. Repeat the process.

When you get him far enough back that he wants to put his head on your side of the trailer, take your fingers and push them against the side of his face or his nose to keep his nose facing forward, while you ask him to break at the poll two inches. Don't worry about trying to get his feet to move, you are only going move his nose. The horse will move his feet to relieve his neck, which has become uncomfortable because his nose is in an awkward position. It's important that you only ask him to move his nose two inches, because you are only trying to get his feet to move two inches at a time.

Q. *When my horse is in the front of a stock trailer, I can't get him to back all the way out.*

A. Don't ask him to back all the way out of the trailer until you've worked through the whole lesson. When you want to teach him to back out, go through the process of loading and unloading one foot, then two feet, having him step in, then out of the trailer.

When you get ready to load three feet, step up in the trailer with him, stop his forward motion, pet him and back his three feet off the trailer. Then, for all four feet, step up in there with him so he doesn't walk up to the front of the trailer. Stop him so his back feet just barely get in the trailer, let him stand, then have him back out.

Then, each time you can let him go farther to the front, and back him out, until you can have him back out the length of the trailer.

Q. *What do I do if I have to load a horse in a hurry, and he's not really trained to lead well?*

A. Those situations are far more unusual than people think. But, if you are in a situation where you need to load a horse who's not trained to lead well enough that he won't drag you off or potentially get away from you, rather than use a halter, attach the lead rope to one ring of a snaffle bit. That way you have more control of the horse. There's no danger to the horse's mouth as long as you don't jerk on the rope. ■PH

Section IV

Putting Theory
Into Practice

19

It Was Worth The Try

*Te was nine years old, afraid of people
and hadn't been handled since he was a weanling,
until Dan decided to try.*

What is so exciting about a guy petting a horse in a round pen? It's exciting when the guy built his own portable round pen and planned the training of this horse for an entire year. And it's especially exciting when the previous owner had given up hope because the horse was considered to be too wild.

The horse is a nine-year-old registered Quarter Horse gelding of impeccable bloodlines, whose dam sold for $25,000. "Te" originally was a gift to a woman who became seriously ill before she could train him. He waited in a 10-acre pasture for her to recover, but she was not able to even walk out to him. He fared just fine on acres of lush pasture with natural shelter and feed supplied in the winter.

Several years ago, a friend of the family attempted to "break" Te. The plan was to lasso him and not let go. The lasso part went OK, but after 450 yards of hanging on at a dead run, the friend changed his plan to "let go and come what may." The horse soon shed the lariat and was left in peace for a few more years.

Then another friend decided it was time to "show that horse who's boss." His idea was to get the horse in a stall, put a saddle on him and climb aboard. He managed to get the saddle on, but that's as far as it went.

Enter Dan. Dan knew about John Lyons' methods and decided this was the way to train this horse. Dan purchased the horse and began planning, dreaming of the day Te would be a great roping horse.

Dan teaches Te the outside turn in the round pen he built.

Te stayed in the same field he had been in for years, but Dan and his wife built a little barn and a round pen, laboring after work and on weekends. After a year's preparation, all was ready. Dan set up the pen on a level spot in the middle of the horse's pasture and got the horse in the pen in only five minutes. This would be easy! Well...maybe not.

After several hours, the horse would face him but not allow Dan to touch him. Dan tried to follow the round-pen lessons, but at the end of the day, they let Te out of the pen. Dan went home to call a trainer he knew who uses Lyons methods and asked for ideas. Dan wanted the trainer to watch and coach him, but Dan wanted to do the work himself.

Another try

Getting the horse into the round pen the next time took nearly two hours. Dan worked another two hours trying to touch the horse and was able to touch him only about six times very briefly. Finally, he asked the trainer for advice. She told him that he had made a good start, as the horse was responding to the cues for inside and outside turns. But Dan was obviously at a stalemate.

After 15 minutes of play-by-play coaching, Dan could pet Te on the face every time he tried. In an hour Dan was rubbing Te's face and ear, and within two hours Dan could run his hands over Te to his rump and all along his sides. What made the difference? The trainer fills us in:

Dan did a good job working the horse going left, then right, then outside and inside turns. With the horse stopping and looking at Dan consistently, Dan started to approach him, intending to work up to petting him.

But, instead of the horse continuing to look at Dan, he turned his head away, as if he was planning to leave. Dan backed off, as was the right thing to do. But, when this happened a number of times, the horse learned Dan would back off when he pulled his head away. Dan wasn't in control — the horse was controlling Dan.

Most people are a little too assertive when working with their horse in the round pen. **Dan was doing the right thing, playing it extra safe, but this was one time he needed to be a little more assertive — to force the horse to make a decision.**

So, the next time Dan tried to approach the horse, instead of backing off as Te withdrew his head, Dan continued toward him to get him to commit to either staying or moving away.

Te stayed and allowed Dan to get closer to him, although he was not looking at Dan. Dan immediately backed away to reward the horse and asked Te to face him again. (This was working on the principle of getting a response, then building on it — not expecting the full response at first.)

He worked through this scenario until the horse didn't take his head away as Dan approached and eventually stood to have his face petted. Of course, he wasn't consistent about it, so when the horse left, Dan asked him to move around the pen a time or two.

In order to overcome his fear of Dan approaching, the horse needed more motivation to stand still. **(The motivation must be greater than the horse's fear, or he sees no reason to make a change.)** After a few times, Te learned that if he took his head away, Dan had him move around the pen, doing inside and outside turns. But if he kept looking at Dan, Dan allowed him to stand and didn't overwhelm him. The horse's fear level went down. It was a turning point in the horse's training — the control shifted back to Dan

Dan theoretically could have worked through this without help, but since there was a Lyons-knowledgeable person nearby, he asked for help, which was wise. If help wasn't available, Dan would probably have figured it out. **He'd have gone back to a point**

Te was worth the try.

in the training where he could ask the horse to do something and have him do it consistently and built the lesson again from there.

Dan's father, sort of a tough-guy type, had been watching the whole time and had tears in his eyes. He just kept shaking his head in disbelief at the "miracle." The previous owner came to see how it was going and was flabbergasted to see Dan petting Te all over. Dan felt a great sense of accomplishment. The trainer felt proud — this is what it's all about — helping someone achieve their dream. ▣

Our thanks to contributing writer Kathy Huggins.

20

Focus On Driving

*Incorporating Lyons techniques
into her training program has helped
world-class driver Keady Cadwell
improve communication with her horses.*

Although the sport of combined driving is barely 25 years old in the United States, it is a rapidly growing discipline that appeals to all ages and equestrian backgrounds. Similar to the three-day event (combined training), a combined driving event (CDE) includes a formal phase (dressage), an endurance phase (marathon) and a final test of accuracy and obedience (cones).

Introduction

J. Keady Cadwell, of Unionville, Pa., and Southern Pines, N.C., is regarded as one of the country's top drivers, having represented the U.S. Equestrian Team at the 1993 World Pairs Championships and being named as team alternate for the 1994 World Four-In-Hand Championships. The entire Cadwell family, including Keady's younger sisters, Miranda and Susan, who crew and navigate during competition, are involved in riding and driving.

In the summer of 1995, Keady was making a strong bid for the 1996 World Four-In-Hand Championships team when disaster struck during a training session at home. A bridle broke on a wheeler (in a four-in-hand, the two horses in front are called leaders, and the rear horses are wheelers). Her father and grandfather dismounted from the carriage to try to fix it, but the horses bolted and tried to turn across a bridge toward home. Instead, they went over the side.

"We were airborne," Keady said. "Two of my horses got badly hurt, and they eventually had to be retired."

• This left Keady without a team, her World Championship hopes destroyed.

Keady has now put together a new team of young horses. She has also installed a round pen on her North Carolina farm and gets help from John Lyons whenever he has a clinic nearby. We talked to Keady about the techniques she learned from John.

Perfect Horse: *Do you both ride and drive the horses?*

Cadwell: Yes. Most of the horses do everything. During the winter, we take them to jumper shows just for a change of pace. And, all of them have fox-hunted.

PH: *How did you become interested in the Lyons' clinics?*

Cadwell: My sister Miranda is my navigator, but she also drives. She likes to teach horses tricks, and she wanted to go to a clinic. So, she signed up with one of my Dutch horses who was part of my World Championships team. We did the symposium and then the riding clinic.

PH: *What was your goal?*

Cadwell: One of our horses has a problem with crowds. Although he had been to the World Championships, he would get in front of a big crowd and lose his mind; he'd just forget what he was supposed to do. It made dressage more than just a little difficult!

PH: *How did he do in the clinic?*

Cadwell: We did a lot of work on bending, "giving to the bit," which was what he needed, because he would see people and just forget everything.

PH: *Did he have a problem with the crowd there?*

Cadwell: He did at one point. Randi (Miranda) was riding him. John was standing in the middle of the ring holding onto him (all 17.1 hands), trying to get him to "give to the bit." John wasn't going to release the rein until he softened, and it took about 20 minutes. He just locks his jaw and won't give to you at all.

PH: *So the answer is...*

Cadwell: Wait him out. It can be frustrating because he's usually good in warm-up, but then he gets in the ring and locks up. I just have to take the slack out of the rein and wait until he gives.

PH: *When you're driving, how do you take a firm hold with him and not interfere with the teammate he's hooked next to?*

Cadwell: We adjust the reins and shorten the connection so it doesn't affect the other horse.

PH: *Have you worked with John and the horses in harness?*

Cadwell: Yes. We took a pair up to Raleigh, and John drove them. He worked a lot on bending, getting them to give to the bit at the walk and trot, bending, bending, and then he ended up galloping

The most challenging and exciting phase of combined driving is the marathon.

204 ■ THE MAKING OF A PERFECT HORSE

them around in a circle, flat out! My Swedish horse had never been in an indoor arena in his whole life; he was very well behaved about it all.

John also worked on correcting a problem with head rubbing. When they stand still, they like to rub their heads on each other.

PH: *Is there any real difference in John's training techniques for riding as opposed to driving?*

Cadwell: Not really. John says that we (drivers) more easily understand what he's talking about, because all we have are the reins. We can't use our body or legs.

PH: *Have you changed any of your training techniques since working with John?*

Cadwell: I try to ask with the bit first and then with the voice, instead of asking with the voice first. John says if we ask with the voice first, we're losing the chance to train our horses from the bit. We use a chirp to make them stop, but John says to ask them from the bit first. Vocal commands aren't as efficient.

PH: *You have horses that have been in international competition. Why do you take them back to the round pen?*

Cadwell: Mostly to get them to focus, teaching them to turn to the inside, come, follow and look to us for direction. We've taken all of our horses back to the round pen — Zaphier, who's been to four World Championships, to the new guys. Generally, John's techniques reinforce the same objectives we need in a good driving horse, which is why we gave Randi a round pen for her birthday this year.

Here, all our paddocks come off the barn. When we bring them in, we just open the door and let them walk in, so we like for them to be very polite in the barn. They all get handled with just a lead shank around the neck, so it's pretty much all the same stuff we've done; we just took it another step further with the round pen.

PH: *Do you work them in the round pen every day?*

Cadwell: At first, it was every day, but now it's just when they need it. If they are not behaving well, or not being obedient on the lead shank, they go back to the round pen.

The object of the cones course is to test the horses' suppleness, energy and obedience.

I walk in, take their halter off, and let them go. They trot forward, then I teach them to turn toward me. Once they are looking at me, focusing on me, guessing what I want by my body language — that's the objective.

That's the whole thing, they pay attention. They learn to read body language and realize that they need to learn to do what I ask; they take me seriously.

PH: *A lot of round pens have solid sides, but yours don't.*

Cadwell: I want them to see everything but still focus on me. At shows we can't shield them from distractions. There's a lot of activity around, and they still need to focus on me.

PH: *What do you mean by focus? A driving horse has a blinker bridle on, so he can't see you.*

Cadwell: They listen. The ears come back. I can call their names individually, and their ears flip back. People say, "Horses don't know their names"...they know their names. They're listening all the time.

Driving multiples, you can see them constantly turning their ears back, trying to listen.

PH: *Any other effects or benefits from work in the round pen?*

Cadwell: One little Thoroughbred was aggressive; he would come into the middle and get right on top of me. I kept working him until he learned to respect my space. When I step toward him, I want him to step back.

One of my Swedish horses was awful in the stall. He would pin his ears, head for the back of the stall and kick at you. Someone must've gotten after him. So after work in the round pen, he turns to face you when you come in the stall.

PH: *What other Lyons techniques do you use?*

Cadwell: We've used the trailer-loading techniques on our younger horses. We had a Thoroughbred who wouldn't step into the wash rack. We taught him to go into the wash stall in about 25 minutes using the trailer-loading technique — no hitting, no rearing, just tap, tap, tap until they take a step forward. Then stop tapping and pet them. Step up, then step down, up, then down. It's a nice, quiet method and always successful; you just have to take the time to do it.

I even came back from the clinic in Raleigh and taught my old event mare to lie down — just for fun. It took me 45 minutes the first time, but now she does it in five minutes.

PH: *You've made the U.S. Equestrian Team, won national events at the advanced level, mastered the round-pen techniques and driven and ridden with John in clinics. Will you continue to participate in John's clinics?*

Cadwell: Yes, even if we can't participate, we love to watch. His whole attitude toward horses is what we like. PH

Our thanks to contributing writer Sue Smithson.

Index

B
back 42, 49, 171, 177, 185, 187, 193, 194

bit 119, 121

bite 33, 65, 66, 181

body language 26, 36, 50, 205

bridle 85, 105

C
cinchy 65, 68, 87

connect the rein to the hip 84, 94

control 21, 35, 55, 63, 66, 94, 97, 110, 143, 144, 148, 180, 199

cue 25, 28, 36, 45, 63, 78, 101, 108, 127, 130, 172, 185, 187

E
emotional control 49

emotions 51, 74, 182

F
fear 22, 52, 62, 73, 74, 77, 79, 80, 85, 120, 176, 192

G
give to pressure 190

give to the bit 51, 100, 105, 125, 131 144, 146, 164, 202

go forward 25, 33, 167, 170, 171, 173, 175, 177, 186, 187

goal 47, 50, 56, 86, 102, 127

H
headshy 52, 84

K
kiss 25, 32, 35, 37, 41, 42, 44, 50, 54, 76

L
lead 45, 170, 175, 194

leg protection 24, 31

lesson 34, 38, 49, 50, 54, 56, 63, 69, 75, 83, 86, 164, 167

locked up 53, 88

lunge 27

lunge line 80

M
minute game 187

motivator 22, 107, 109

P
pain 23, 24, 119, 121

performance 22

pulling back 52, 190

putting pressure on the hip 27

putting pressure on the nose 27

R
rears 129, 181

rein 121, 146, 204

release 108, 111

replacement concept 113

ride 83, 92, 94, 109

round pen 11, 19, 31, 53, 63, 83, 145, 197, 204

rule 28, 33, 50, 79, 145

S

sacking out 51, 62, 63, 70, 74, 76, 77, 83, 86

saddling 59, 63, 64, 68

safe 11, 19, 20, 63, 73, 76, 130, 178, 190

snaffle 119

spook in place 73, 84

stop 39, 41, 100, 122, 125, 178, 180

T

tie 174, 187, 189

For information regarding *John Lyons' Perfect Horse*,
the monthly magazine, see our web site www.perfecthorse.com
or call the publisher, Belvoir Publications, Inc. at 800-424-7887.

PHOTO CREDIT: MARK WALPIN, CHARLES HILTON, MAUREEN GALLATIN
BOOK DESIGN AND LAYOUT: SUSAN R. TOMKIN